PRAISE FOR

MECHANICS OF AWAKENING

"Thirty years ago, while on a year long sabbatical in Hawaii, Gary Sherman underwent a life-changing personal transformation. Although he was already a skilled meditator and therapist, the level of knowledge and awareness transmitted to him during this period was revelatory. Ever since, he and his wife Ellen have been skillfully teaching others how to gain this awareness for themselves and how to integrate it into their daily lives. I personally have benefited from this teaching, and now, with this book in hand, I can continue to do so."

—Amy L. Lansky, Ph.D, Author of *Active Consciousness: Awakening the Power Within* and *Impossible Cure*

"I love a book that I can put down frequently, not just to ponder but to experience and personally test the truths I have just awakened to in the reading, especially as they apply to the evolving nature of my own life. So I am grateful for this book. By offering a practice for self-awareness and self-creation, it has become a life changer for me, a thriller about the nature of my own consciousness. I'll be turning to it often."

—Pierre Delattre, Author of *Tales of the Dali Lama*, *Walking on Air* and *Episodes*

"Gary Sherman has accomplished a spectacular feat in this book. He not only describes the inner and outer dimensions of our perception of reality, the upper and lower energetic resonances of consciousness within the mind, emotions and the physical body but also gives us very clear exercises to help us ground this knowledge into our ever-evolving self. It is one of the clearest books I have ever read concerning these matters. I highly recommend it."

—Warren Bellows, Acupuncturist, Artist and Author of
*Floral Acupuncture: Applying the flower essences
of Dr. Bach to acupuncture sites*

"Gary Sherman has written a truly insightful and helpful book that will positively change the lives of its readers. Although many books have wise teachings, few have accessible, reliable and transformative practices like this one. I highly recommend this book."

—Russell Delman, Founder of
The Embodied Life School

"The power of this book lies not only in the beauty and precision of its language, but that the words come *alive*. The book causes in me what it teaches. Very few books can do that! In the process of reading *The Mechanics of Awakening* you awaken."

—Silvia Reischl, Founder of
The Reischl Method of Functional Healing

The Mechanics of Awakening

PERCEPTUAL INTEGRATION

THE MECHANICS OF AWAKENING

Gary Sherman

Inner Harmonics Press
Cotati, California

Inner Harmonics Press

P.O. Box 479

Cotati, CA 94931

For more information, contact: Inner Harmonics Press

Email: Innerharmonicspress@gmail.com

Also visit www.mechanicsofawakening.com for information about the content of this book.

Library of Congress Control Number: 2013947677

ISBN-13: 978-1-886594-17-3

ISBN-10: 1-886594-17-1

First printing September 2013

Cover and interior art: Ellen Miller, ellenmillerart.com

Cover and text design by Bookwrights, bookwrights.com

To Ellen – my constant light.

CONTENTS

PREFACE

One afternoon in the summer of 1987 I was walking from my home office on my way to the kitchen to make myself some lunch. As I walked, I was following a thought in my mind about a client I had just seen in session. As I followed my train of thought, in mid-sentence, it stopped abruptly and I heard the words *perceptual integration* inserted into the middle of the sentence, and then the rest of the normal preceding thought continued to its completion. I stopped in confusion. Having sat in meditation for many years, I had a deep respect for the independent nature of thought. I recognized that most of the time I was the receiver of thought and not the thinker. But to have a couple of words placed in the middle of a non-related sentence, as if placed there on purpose was very disconcerting. It's not a stretch to say that all of us believe our thoughts are private even though we have little awareness of how they are sourced.

It was such an odd experience that I quickly entered the house and shared the experience with my wife Ellen. The way these words had appeared out of nowhere and out of context, left no option but to hear them. I found the term intriguing but with no apparent meaning. For a while the words lingered in my awareness, then were forgotten. Little did I know that an adventure in consciousness was being initiated and the words perceptual integration were the herald announcing its beginning.

The self we inhabit is a marvelous and mysterious construction. As a psychotherapist and teacher of meditation and self-awareness for over forty years, I have been challenged with exploring its nature and answering this question: How can we learn about our self from ourselves? Can the very act of being who we are also be a conscious learning experience that expands and evolves us, generates new depths of understanding and perception, and connects us with the essence of who we are? Over the years, I have found our capacity to be self-aware at the heart of this question.

The scientific version of our physical beginning as a species proposes that a few million years ago, our early ancestors left the cover of the forest, spread out over the open savanna, started walking upright, evolved a larger brain, and at some point in this process became self-aware creatures. The metaphysical view of our evolution sees us as soul, projecting ourselves into physical form. From this point of view, we have always been engaged in a self-aware process of becoming.

Both points of view taken together represent our unique nature. Science represents our objective interface with reality, while metaphysics represents our subjective experience. Whether by accident or design, we are graced with the capacity to know both sides of the coin. We can know our inner world and our outer world equally.

Beyond our stories about how we arrived here, we are self-aware creatures. This capacity is a wonderful aspect of our nature. It allows us the ability to explore the self beyond the familiar boundaries we use and accept to know ourselves. As we experience ourselves as both subject and object, we can witness the birth of ourselves in each moment, and discover how we work and who we are. We can develop the capacity to elevate our encounter with our self beyond instinct and habit to a consciously aware process. *It can be argued that this capacity for self-awareness is the most essential ingredient that makes us human and is at the heart of our essence, a point of view I follow throughout this book.*

First, I am writing this book to offer evidence for the belief that within our normal everyday lives there exists the capacity for greater self-awareness and expanded perception. I draw from my own experience, as well as the experience of my students throughout the years, to construct a first-person narrative that explores the process of living deeply within your self in such a way that you learn about your self from yourself as a conscious process.

Secondly, I describe a process of fundamental shifts in attention and perception that generate the experience of living in *a state of self-awareness*. We are all born with the capacity for self- awareness. Whether we cultivate this attribute and explore its nature and it's possibility for being is another matter. Having self-awareness and being in a state of self-awareness are two different orders of experience, a distinction I make and encourage us to follow.

I begin by sharing my personal experience of an expansion in consciousness that began with my walk from my office to the kitchen described earlier.

Where it led changed my life and introduced me to

the broader possibilities that underlie our normal every-day life. This personal experience is important to share be-cause it speaks to a more multidimensional view of the self, and lays the foundation for the approach I take throughout the book.

Next, I address the process of cultivating self-aware-ness as a conscious practice within everyday life. Using my personal experience and the knowledge garnered from many others, I outline a way to practice skills in aware-ness that will open you to greater possibilities for expand-ed perception.

Utilizing these skills for becoming self-aware brings us to the practice of how to stabilize our state of being while being subject to the ups and downs we encounter in everyday life. Can self-awareness contribute to a more graceful experience of our thoughts, feelings and behav-iors? I answer this question by sharing a short course of practices that will serve to support you in managing your state of being more effectively and also open you to a more expanded state of consciousness.

Finally, I leave you with the vision that exercising your natural capacity for self-awareness will lead to a funda-mental shift in consciousness and initiate a marvelous journey that will transform your life and imbue it with meaning and wonder. My hope is that this book inspires you to step into yourself more deeply and begin the process of learning about your self from yourself, a journey that will take you into the essence of who you are.

PART ONE

INITIATION

CHAPTER 1

MEETING THE SPEAKER

My journey on the path of self-awareness had its most auspicious and profound opening in the late 1980's amongst the sun drenched beaches and tropical forests of paradise. As I call up those memories, I am infused with the excitement and energy that characterized this time in my life.

My wife Ellen and I were settling into the house we had just rented on the island of Maui in Hawaii. After hopping from one island to the next looking for a good place to live for a year, the house we found on the side of Mt. Haleakala was perfect. At an altitude of 2000 feet, we were guaranteed cool afternoons and brisk nights. We could look out over the west side of the island and see the blue Pacific Ocean. Walking out on the deck each morning, I was surrounded by deep red and purple bougainvillea and ripe papayas waiting to be plucked. We were relatively secluded, yet in easy reach of beaches and up country haunts of interest. We had finally come to rest. It was January 2, 1988.

Months before we had come to the decision to take a mid-life break. We had been living on the campus of Stanford University in Palo Alto, California in a house we loved. We had been working hard for many years and now wanted to wake up in the morning with no pre-existing structure determining how our day should unfold. Our goal was to stop our forward momentum, shed past and future projections and come to rest in the present. No structure and no future.

Four years had passed since Ellen had suffered a rare form of fungal pneumonia that had threatened her life. She was well now and she wanted to fulfill a commitment she made to herself when hospitalized. While sitting on her hospital bed, she had experienced a voice deep inside her suggesting that it was time for her to seek more quiet in her life. In response to this voice, she committed herself to making this possible. We were finally fulfilling her promise.

We put our current work life on hold. I took a sabbatical from my busy practice as a psychotherapist after making sure all my clients would be receiving good care in my absence. Ellen did the same with her counseling practice. We sold our cars, put the rest of our belongings in storage and off we went with just a few boxes of essentials.

We were viewing this retreat as a time for us to explore our relationship with each other as well as deepening our relationship with ourselves outside the demands of our current life. We wanted to retreat with each other and follow where it would take us. We both had been pursuing our interest in exploring deeper states of consciousness for many years through meditation practice and were looking forward to creating the time and space to explore this interest further.

One morning, a month after settling into the new house, we began a morning sitting together. We often sat together in meditation, using a practice of stating our experience to each other as we shifted our attention to deeper states. By now we always sat with a tape recorder running, just in case there was anything said during our sittings we wanted to hear again. After a few minutes of quieting down, something unusual began to take place.

As I became quiet within myself, I suddenly began to experience an expansion of consciousness. Internally, I felt a sense of expanding in all directions with a simultaneous lifting upward. This was not an out of body experience. I could still feel my body residing in the middle of this expanding field and felt present within it. At the same time, I also felt present in the field as well. I say field because my attention was not localized and targeting any particular aspects of my experience, or moving from one to the other, but instead, holding all of its content equally in place and in a wonderfully profound harmony and congruence. It was a *multidimensional experience.*

As the expansive movement continued, my field of perception became more rarified, as my very being quickened and oscillated at a higher frequency. My normal sense of embodiment was replaced by a pervasive sense of size, with no definite boundaries. As the upward movement subsided, my experience became stabilized as a profoundly open, transparent, quiet and still field of perception.

Sitting as this field of open awareness, I felt an impulse to speak. I felt a welling up of energy that had its own direction and purpose. I knew instinctively that I would have to let go in order to allow it to happen. I surrendered to the impulse, opened my mouth and began to speak.

My first words were: "Perceptual Integration has as one of its components the introduction of new perceptions into conscious awareness. This is the act you are presently engaged in. An aspect of this process of integration is allowing subtle perceptions to become real for you. It is allowing your inner senses to play freely at the surface of your awareness. The opening of these sensed impressions allows for an expansion and freedom to experience qualities of a deeper Self that are always present yet unseen. They exist just beneath normal perception."

The speaking continued for another ten minutes and then ended with: "Perceptual Integration, as this term is being used here, is to move the center of experience from the external to the internal, which then serves to expand perception."

As the speaking ended, my attention was drawn back to my body. Upon opening my eyes, I found myself sitting in the room I had left minutes before. I sat there quietly, with the most profound sense of completeness I had ever experienced in my life, a feeling of coming home. It was as if something in me that I had wanted to express my whole life had finally been released. I felt full, complete and whole.

While the speaking was taking place I was completely conscious. My thoughts were tracking the direction it was taking and then suddenly hit a crossroads of meaning; my thoughts went left and the speaking went right, following a more profound vein of understanding that ran under the surface of my experience. It was a very unusual experience and, at its heart, one that produced a wonderful sense of alignment and grace.

As we sat sharing our experience of what had just happened, I remembered the event that had occurred months before while walking through my backyard and hearing the words perceptual integration. Now, still reverberating with the energy of the experience, it seemed as if there was no time between the occurrence of that thought and this speaking; it had resurfaced and was about to make it's meaning known.

I got up from my chair, still in the afterglow of the experience and walked out onto the deck of the house. Standing by the railing, my view flowed down the mountain and out into the blue Pacific waters. As my sight wandered through the terrain and down to the sea, my mind kept noticing each discrete object my eyes fell upon— grass, trees, flowers, earth, mountain, sky, houses, roads, cars, people, etc. I already had a category for how I was to perceive everything I saw. In the moment that I registered this insight, my attention was pulled into an interior space, just past my thoughts and sensations, that was full and rich with experience my mind had no language for. A voice inside this space said, "This is the space of newness and creativity. You see that your outer perception is full and known. The inside of you waits to be explored. It is open and accessible to direct perception. This is where you will find what you are looking for, the completion of the self you know."

The next morning the experience of expansion and speaking repeated itself during our sitting. Each morning from then on we sat in meditation; I was moved into an elevated state and began speaking about a multidimensional view of human consciousness. I was told it was time for humanity to broaden its view of reality to include those dimensions of experience that went unseen or unrecognized because of our limited perception of what we considered real. As one morning followed another, a body of knowledge large in scope and deep in its understanding was delivered. The experience repeated itself for fifty-two days and then stopped. What transpired between its beginning and ending transformed us forever.

CHAPTER 2

IN PREPARATION

Hindsight certainly lends itself to revealing the larger patterns that bring us to the present moment. As I look back over the arc of my life, I see the interplay of interest, decision and circumstance that prepared me for my experience in Maui.

I was fortunate enough to mature into young adulthood in the sixties and seventies and, like thousands in my generation, had embraced the search for new paradigms for living and being. My interest in being a psychotherapist had brought me to graduate school at the University of Southern California. I had always been interested in people, human nature and what makes us who we are. My own chaotic childhood, my parents' divorce and frequent moves, caused me a good deal of suffering. I was interested in removing the pain and lack of self-confidence that characterized my experience. By learning to help others, I hoped I would learn to help myself as well.

One day, while still an undergraduate and floundering over what to do after graduation, my sister visited my parents' house while I was there.

She started talking about her relationship with her husband. I sat and listened. Every now and then I would ask her a question to better understand where she was coming from.

After a while she turned to me and said, "You know, you are a really good listener. You should think about doing it for a living." Her feedback offered me a new direction. Upon graduation I applied to the USC Graduate School of Social Work. It was 1968. Just the time to take advantage of the political, social and cultural revolution being expressed through sex, drugs and rock 'n roll. When the introduction of Eastern spirituality hit American culture, I was primed to receive it.

I was living in the Hollywood Hills above Los Angeles at the time. My roommate's girlfriend had been to the house and accidently left a book on Zen Buddhism in the kitchen. I was surprised by my own interest in picking it up. I didn't come from a religious background; I had only been in a church twice. When my parents were separated, my father, for some reason known only to him, wanted us to be baptized together. After attending the local Methodist Church twice, they put us under the water, one after the other. While this was meaningful for my father, it left me with no interest in returning. Later in college, I began to adopt a scientific point of view, which supported my interests in the social and behavioral sciences. Not only did I lack interest in religion, I held the view that the institutions and ideologies that sprang from the original revelations that underlay religion were responsible for much of the misunderstandings and suffering in the world.

When I opened the book on Zen Buddhism and began leafing through the pages, I became absorbed. They weren't talking about God. They were talking about the possibility of bringing about a transformation in your own consciousness through your own effort. Just like the light that went on when my sister gave me my future work, this light infused me in a deeper way.

After reading the book, I started picking up other books about spirituality, metaphysics, philosophy and consciousness. Following a year of intense reading, I had worked my way from ancient Greece to New Age writing that was emerging around this time. I found essentially the same message, repeated over and over again in all the writings, regardless of the particular path being described or its historical context, i.e., that concept alone could not create a shift in consciousness. Having the idea was not the thing itself. To facilitate a shift one had to meet the self in direct experience and observe how it was brought into being. While desire and intent were of critical importance, it was the activation of awakened self-awareness that prepared one for the experience. Some form of meditation practice was always sited as a method for achieving this end.

I began to engage with the practice of meditation, sometimes stopping my life for long periods in order to study and practice within a structured environment. Sometimes I found myself drawn to the practices in different traditions. However, whether it was Eastern or Western schools of thought or practice, I was always aware that what these traditions offered was removed from the original revelations that inspired them. I would only later recognize how important it was for me to make my own direct contact with higher consciousness, and generate my own understandings of its meaning and consequence for human beingness. An inner imperative kept me from following any particular tradition, sometimes leaving me without the support of like-minded others, which can be so important while attempting shifts in perception and consciousness.

I met my partner in life and future wife, Ellen, while engaged in one of these periods of study. It is impossible to know what direction my life might otherwise have taken, but in meeting Ellen, I met someone as deeply committed as I was to unraveling the mystery behind the life we live. Together we shared extraordinary experiences and made mutual decisions that resulted in our sitting across from one another, in a house on the side of a volcano in Hawaii, sharing an unusual and wonderful experience.

As the years passed, I had many experiences in meditation that introduced me to the subtle energies beyond the conscious mind and the hard fact of the physical body. My ideas about my essential nature continued to form and evolve. I was beginning to know myself as a multidimensional being. This was demonstrated to me through a series of powerful dreams that began about a year and a half before we took our mid-life retreat to Hawaii.

What follows is a description of one of the dreams in this series and the events that followed it. The dream began this way. I am aware of being in a large metropolitan area, high up, overlooking tall buildings. The look of the city immediately gives me the sense that I am viewing a time frame not my own – it is more like New York City in the late 1800s. I am moving over the tops of buildings, looking down, as if I am a bird in flight. I see a man with an easel painting on the rooftop of one of the buildings. My view moves closer to him and I empathically know that he is somehow connected to me. While he doesn't resemble me physically, I know that we are connected in identity. As soon as I have this recognition, I am made aware of his point of view and begin to experience the joy he is having in painting. As the dream unfolds, I experience the knowledge that this is another *me* in a different time frame. Just as I am realizing that I have a larger identity through time, I wake up. I immediately wake Ellen and tell her about the dream.

Walking through the house a few days later, I see a bag of clay that Ellen had purchased some months earlier. Until this time I had never been interested in art. I took the clay, set up a table in our screened-in side porch, and began to play.

For many weeks, I came home from work and immediately sat down with the clay. I was aware that something out of the ordinary was happening because of the energy and intensity I felt while doing it. Every now and then Ellen came out to the porch to take a peek at what I was doing and was utterly amazed. I started with a ball of clay the size of a human head and began to form it. It first took the shape of a Neanderthal male, quite striking with its broad forehead and massive bone structure.

Every couple of days I saw the head change as I re-worked it. It seemed as though I was taking the form through historical stages. The Neanderthal became an ab-original-looking man and then a Native American. The head finally emerged as a mustached European male, who had the feel of being from the eighteenth or nineteenth century.

I was deeply engrossed in this process and as soon as I completed the first head, I started another one. When Ellen asked me what I was experiencing I said, "I don't know, I just sit down in front of the clay and let my hands lead." Over the next few months I created three heads. Each was wonderfully alive, full of energy and strangely familiar to me. Each succeeding head was more accomplished than the one before. The second piece was a beautiful African woman, the third, a bust of a wise-looking Asian man.

A friend, who was visiting when the first head was completed, said the piece was as accomplished as the sculp-ture in a museum exhibit he had just seen. I had no con-scious thoughts about what I was doing; I just allowed my hands to create and in the process, I created the works of an accomplished artist. I knew as I worked the clay that something extraordinary was happening. It wasn't just an artistic interest I was acting out, but a deeply felt urge to allow my hands to express themselves through the clay. I was experiencing split awareness. I was both intensely in-volved and, at the same time, a witness to a process that was unfolding before my eyes. My experience was one of wonder and joy.

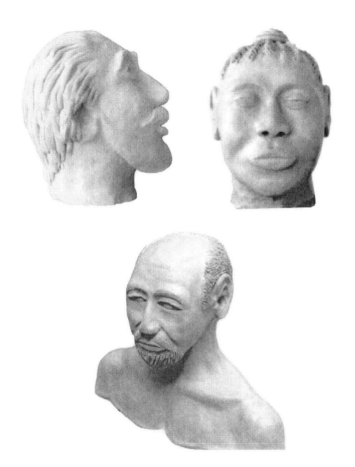

By the time I had sculpted all three heads, I knew that this was a continuation, in the waking state, of something that had transpired in my dream with the artist. This artist part of myself had imbued me with his gift of expression. Now, I was acting it out and making it my own. I was also aware that the heads I was sculpting were emotionally related to me, as was the artist in the dream. In some form, they were my selves. What most amazed me about the whole experience was that an act, which had taken form in a dream state, had completed itself in my waking moments. The separation between my dreaming self, my waking self and other dimensions of my greater identity were collapsing and creating a transparency that would surface still further in the speaking experience in Hawaii.

CHAPTER 3

THE SPEAKING

s I described in Chapter 1, the speaking began while sitting in meditation one morning. It happened quickly and suddenly. One minute I was settling into feeling my body and letting my thoughts pass by without engaging them. Then after a few minutes, I began to feel a lifting feeling that was different than the downward sensation I usually felt when letting go of thought and relaxing into the body.

I surrendered to this feeling of lifting, and allowed myself to enjoy the lightness and intrinsic sense of expanding upward that continued to occur. After a few minutes, the lifting feeling stabilized; I found myself resting as an infinitely large field of awareness that was empty, yet full at the same time. While I was aware that my body occupied space within this field, I experienced my attention more identified as the field. My conscious mind and my body were present, but this was secondary to the incredible aliveness that the field enjoyed as itself.

As I sat as this field of awareness, I experienced a quickening and felt the impulse to speak. At first I was reluctant to let go. Then I relaxed my hold on the movement, opened my mouth and started speaking. My first statement was, "Perceptual Integration has as one of its components the introduction of new perceptions into conscious awareness. This is the act you are presently engaged in."

I had no idea what perceptual integration meant or what it referred to. I felt like I had tuned into some broadcast that was available to me in this elevated state of consciousness. It felt both personal and impersonal as it addressed my current experience as well as a larger process of consciousness that had meaning far beyond my personal experience.

Throughout the fifty-two days of the speaking, I had no clue as to its source. The only concepts I could apply to the experience were the psychological or spiritual ideas I had been exposed to. Either I was dissociating, or channeling my higher self, a guide, or another disembodied being. I would later understand that not knowing created the necessary space that allowed the joining to occur. Knowing the source would have been a hindrance, burdening me with expectations and preconceived ideas into which I would have tried to fit my new experience.

Each morning we would wake up, shower and eat, and then begin our sitting. I had no idea if the experience would continue after the first morning. But each morning as we sat in meditation, it would happen. After three such mornings, we decided to stop recording the sessions. The speaking would occur for about 20 minutes; we quickly saw that transcribing the sessions would be a big job. Instead, for the rest of the sittings, Ellen sat at the computer, while in her own elevated state, and typed everything that was said. This was a virtuoso performance on her part. She describes it this way, "While in this huge space, I let Gary's words pass through me and out my hands as they moved across the keyboard. This process was only one of many going on. At the same time, I was receiving the conceptual meaning of the words, followed by the direct perception of what they represented as a multidimensional experience."

We would picture it as a triangle; each of us represented the bottom two angles, grounded in the physical dimension, and the apex of the triangle was the source of the speaking. On the fifty-third day, we sat together in the morning and the impulse to speak was gone. Everything that needed to be said had been communicated, and this particular experience was complete.

Now, many years later, I see that, at the time, I didn't fully understand what had actually occurred. This is quite typical of these kinds of experiences where a shift in one's state of awareness leaves the conscious mind behind, unable to make sense of it. While I was quite aware of the many ways in which the experience was impacting us, I didn't understand that the very experience that was being talked about, the process of perceptual integration, was actually happening to both of us. By cooperatively engaging with the source of the speaking, a larger and more refined dimension of ourselves moved forward into conscious awareness, and joined with our everyday selves to produce a shift in consciousness and state of being; this was the same process the speaking was calling a perceptual integration.

The speaking began by talking about the need to bring into awareness the more subtle side of our nature. This subtle aspect of the self, while always operating and present, is a dimension of experience that is often unseen because our attention is usually directed outward into the world or into our thoughts about the world. While this focus is necessary and valid for producing our perception of the world and our place within it, it only allows us to see a limited part of who and what we really are.

This process was described during the speaking as follows:

"Allow these subtle perceptions to become observable and therefore made real for the individual. The opening up of these sensed impressions allows for an expansion and freedom to experience qualities of a deeper self that is always present. While these impressions are always available, it is your desire and interest to expand the self that calls forth these capacities so they can be joined with conscious awareness and become appreciated and utilized as part of the creative unfolding of experience."

When this statement was received, I was sitting in a huge, open field of awareness that was initiated by turning my attention inward. This experience would never have happened if I had been exclusively focused into the external world. As I was shown in Maui, while standing on the deck of our house looking out to the sea, my outer perception was full of what was already known, labeled and conceptualized. There was nothing new to see. In other words, my outer perception was dominated by the habit of conditioned sight. But my inner world and my place within it was waiting to be discovered, waiting to join a world of new experience with the already known self and through this perceptual integration, create a new state of being.

As the speaking continued each day, it became clear why perception was being addressed. It was referred to as a creative meeting place between the deeper subjective parts of the self and the outer perceived reality that we experience as the objective world of sense impressions.

Our outer perception was described as a creative act, not a reflective or passive one. The outer world was seen as a creative projection of consciousness, representing the perceiver's beliefs about reality and materialized as a living framework. The present moment of conscious awareness was being pointed to as the most powerful experience from which to discover, know and transform ourselves.

In normal everyday consciousness we take for granted that what we perceive as "out there" is actually out there and separate from our perception of it. Our job is simply to represent it as accurately as possible. When we do, we are said to have a good grasp on reality.

"We speak of transforming the very perception of self into a new experience. The attempt at the present time for larger aspects of your consciousness to make themselves available is an attempt to create a new understanding that flows from a new configuration of being. Each time you experience a new aspect of your self, by its very presence, it demands a reorganization of how you hold the nature of yourself and of reality. This is a natural process. The universe is alive. Your experience is alive. It is responsive to each event that occurs within the field of which it is a part."

We were being encouraged to be playful and open, and to not succumb to the impulse to judge, correct or problem solve as the mind habitually does.

"We wish to coach you and speak to you about creating for yourself an arena within which experimentation and playfulness can take place. Since in your normal outer experience all space is taken up, used as it were, for those operations you consider consensual reality, we must create a new inner playground. We wish to do this in a reality where time and space have more flexibility. For now we are calling this the arena of perception."

The here and now of our self-experience is a perceptual creation that gives us feedback about the nature and form of our present state. Where our inner experience and our outer perceived reality meet is the location in consciousness where we both receive ourselves and create ourselves simultaneously. From this *point of perception*, we can explore deeper dimensions of the inner self while still being engaged with our outer life.

The speaking went even further:

"It is time for man to begin to understand that all consciousness is cooperative in nature. There are dimensions to human consciousness that contribute to and participate in each perceptive act. It is a multidimensional creation that is contributed to by all levels of the whole self, each receiving energy and giving meaning and fulfillment appropriate to each level of participation. Because you have limited your conscious awareness to only a part of the whole self, you believe that only the self you know is involved in producing each moment of perceived reality."

While this was being stated, my whole field of awareness turned transparent and I could sense/feel many simultaneous dimensions of experience present at the same moment, each contributing to the very point of perception I was resting in. I continued speaking while holding this focus:

"The very fact that you are aware, and that you receive experience in the way you do, is a cooperative effort that goes far beyond your own personally held identity. Since man has seen himself as separate, so his perception has seemed to be his alone. It is time to go beyond this narrow focus to expand and deepen your awareness of the unseen aspects of your own larger consciousness. In order to appreciate the true significance of this sense of wholeness, a new experience must be born, i.e., the actual creativity of the whole as it produces new organization and new structure from the inside out. The external as you know it, only contains what has been reflected out into it from the interior. This is why openings in the fabric of perception are important at this time."

Ellen and I were certainly finding ourselves in the middle of new organization and new structure. We were so flooded with ideas, feelings and capacities in altered perception that our understanding was lagging far behind our experience. Ellen illustrates this with the following comment written at the time:

"Gary and I were in conversation today when I had an experience that is happening a lot lately. I would say something and Gary would become excited and tell me to write it down. When I tried to focus on writing it down, I would go blank. I experienced myself while speaking as very open and non-focused. I felt as if a larger me was rearranging my thoughts so that I was thinking things for the first time, yet didn't understand their meaning. When I tried to focus in to remember what was said, I would go blank. He would have to help me remember and then we could reconstruct it and write it. This was a very interesting experience. It is very exciting to be present at the birth of new thinking."

This of course was the process we were engaged in. A new level of consciousness was being forged and brought into conscious awareness. Old beliefs and points of view were being moved to the side to make room for new, direct experience. Our ability to suspend the need to understand, before an actual experience was allowed to emerge, became a necessary ingredient in the process. We simply had to stay open and keep accepting and trusting that understanding would follow.

Our conscious minds, instead of leading, were being invited to follow and join in a larger process that was informed by a more comprehensive knowing. Parts of the self were being shifted around and taking on new relationships so that an expanded state of being could emerge.

CHAPTER 4

THE CURRENT

As the speaking experience continued over the days that followed, I became more comfortable with allowing it to flow unimpeded. The experiences that always arrived simultaneously with the speaking became clearer. Although Ellen's and my experiences would differ slightly, giving each of us our own unique perception, they were also amazingly similar. We were both touching into the same level of consciousness and engaging with it as a cooperative unit.

Shortly into the speaking, I began to be impacted by what I call *the current*. My normal everyday consciousness began to hum at a different frequency. I felt a current of energy running through my experience that infused me with insight and revelatory content. As it continued, I began carrying a notebook with me wherever I went. At first I thought I could remember the content and write it down later, but then I lost it before I had a chance to record it. I thought my conscious mind could contain the experience and retain it; I didn't recognize that I was downloading information from one state of consciousness to another, and that each level, upon receiving new input, naturally translates it into what it recognizes as meaningful and relevant.

The content was simply too new and subtle for my conscious mind to process. While driving, I often pulled over to the side of the road to safely allow the experience and fully capture the new vision I was seeing. Or, while swimming in the ocean, I had to hurry back to shore so that I could get to my notebook in time to record some inspiration before I lost it.

This wasn't a disruptive or fearful experience. It was soft, yet strong, joyful and insightful, cutting through perceptions that held me in place and restricted my ability to move freely within myself and in the outer world. I found it necessary to stay embodied and retain a good sense of ground in the present moment. The morning sittings provided this ground. While being elevated into a more refined state of consciousness, I always experienced a profound sense of wholeness and balance. The content of the speaking provided a context for what I was experiencing during the day, and gave me a sense of safety and curiosity about what was unfolding.

Having Ellen, who was having a similar experience, as a partner and companion was an enormous support. She also was moved into more expanded states in our morning sittings, and was subject to the same current of inspiration during the day. She was able to meet me in this new state of consciousness, and understand the experience from the inside. We would leapfrog off each other, as well as provide a safety net of reality checks. This was a unique instance of two people encountering a shift in consciousness simultaneously.

I began to realize that I was being rewired from the inside out. In the midst of these infusions of energy, I saw how I was organizing my experience around a particular belief. I was then given a larger view that resolved the inherent limitation of that belief and its impact on me.

The following are some examples of my successes in reaching my notebook in time. They illustrate the impact the current was having on me more clearly than any description I might attempt, since they contain the energy of the moment, and give a direct sense of how some of my issues were being resolved. They also hint at the meaning of *Perceptional Integration*, a term that the speaking kept referring to. This concept pointed to an important dynamic within consciousness, which has to do with an expansion in perception and a shift in the state of the perceiver.

I spend my days seeing how I make things up. I can look at each moment as good or bad, purposeful or without meaning, and I am confronted with having to be the chooser of my circumstance. When I choose to be doing what I am doing, it removes me from the realm of judgment. My first step is to choose what already is, to choose where I am, who I am, and what I am presently doing.

This realization helped me when I fell into moments of doubt and fear about decisions I had made. Walking down to the beach to take a swim one day I heard a voice asking me "What are you doing? Everyone else is working today. You should be too! You have no job, no home and not enough money to support this kind of life style. What have you been thinking?" I would then start to panic and feel like all the choices I had made were invalid, and that I had deluded myself into making a terrible mistake. I became the victim of my past choices. I would stop and say to myself, "Okay. Let's start over from right now. Is this where you want to be and is this what you want to be doing with your life right now? " Framed within that context, I always came to the same conclusion, "Yes, this is exactly what I want." With this clarity, I was able to re-choose what I was already experiencing. The choice transcended the power of my old story to send me into the anguish of self-doubt.

In some areas of my experience, I feel victimized by the world. I think that the world exists outside of my perception of it, as real and objective. All my resignation comes from thinking, conceiving and ultimately perceiving that reality is fixed. I am never resigned in areas of my life where I understand and accept that what I see as reality has only been assigned there by me. When I recognize that the world is only a perception, I have the possibility of affecting it, changing it and recreating it.

I began to see how the current was working on me and attempting to reorganize my experience into a more harmonious state of being. As soon as I felt the current moving through me, I would stop whatever I was doing and make myself available for the new view that followed. I experienced the current as an electrified feeling moving through my body, similar to the feeling of sitting in meditation and feeling the impulse to speak. Often, before I became aware of the current in the body, I found myself in the middle of a new view or conception that lit up my mind. It was as if the mind/body connection was happening simultaneously, cooperating to produce the unifying field of perception that followed.

This is not a unique experience. It happens all the time within normal everyday experience. However, we are often unaware of it and unable to see it for what it is—new material being delivered to the conscious mind, producing what we experience as a vision, inspiration or revelation. This natural, yet often unacknowledged, dynamic is part of the extraordinariness that lies within our ordinary experience.

I recorded the notes below after running from the supermarket, leaving my groceries stranded in the aisle, and rushing for my notebook in the car.

When I choose to give my energy to supporting my intention, I support being free. I used to think my freedom had to do with being free to feel or think whatever I wanted to. When I support my intentions in life, I am supporting my choices, and it is in exercising choice that I find my freedom.

I am seeing that our trip to Hawaii is a conscious experiment in eliminating structure in our lives so that we can understand that freedom from structure is not what matters; it is learning to use structure freely.

This was an important realization for me. In the past I created structures to support my work, my relationships to family and friends, and other commitments that held my life together. Then I would feel burdened by the weight these commitments carried and forget that I was the one who put them in place. Instead of serving me, and they did, I would yearn for unstructured time to pursue those interests and desires that I felt I had no time for.

Having removed all pre-existing structures on our retreat, I saw that manufacturing structure is a part of our nature. It is as natural as breathing. Because we live in time and space, every idea and desire we act out into a perceived future creates the structures that hold it in place as a framework for potential action.

My belief that I was bound by the structures I had created trapped me in a self-created dilemma. Seeing that I could learn to use structure freely resulted in a profound reversal in perception. I was now free to build structures as an outer expression of my inner intentions and desires with the exuberance and joy that comes with creative play. I could also give myself permission to take the structures apart and rearrange them when they didn't represent my current self.

I began to see that the process of perceptual integration was showing me that the external world is the manifested result of our internal conceptions. Integration meant bringing the self and the world into conscious alignment.

I am invested in being continuous. I demand consistency of my reality. In other words, I seem to be committed to sameness, wanting to be surrounded by what is familiar. This is particularly so when it comes to my own self. I want the experience of myself to be stable and constant through time. I achieve this through selective inattention. I keep bringing my past experience into the perception of the present moment in order to create safety and security.

The energy that infused me in these moments of inspiration was attempting to open me up and clear a space for new experience without energizing old limiting conceptions. I later understood this shift in energetic terms. My everyday consciousness was being raised to a new frequency that was more harmonious with the higher frequency represented by the speaking. I was being worked from both ends. My everyday consciousness was being quickened and my higher consciousness was making itself available to my conscious self. I felt I was being prepared to experience a joining or blending of the two energetic frequencies that would result in the birth of a new state of being.

I am aware that I have created my experience in a way that has never allowed me to speak myself freely into the world. I have been constricted and denied myself permission to speak due to my belief that out there was real and substantial, and therefore only able to be represented truthfully when it was described accurately. I have been at the effect of my own conditioning as a western, rational and scientifically trained form of consciousness. I always believed that the fear I had of speaking would disappear once I could reflect the truth accurately or could be okay with being incorrect. I now see clearly that my fear of expressing myself was self-imposed. I didn't understand the true nature of my own being, i.e., that through an act of perception, I generate realities.

All our problems or issues are perceptual in nature. They are the natural and perfect manifestation of our state of consciousness at any given time. How we appear in the world is directly related to how the world appears to us.

When I could, I rode out the current, tracking its ascending arc and its reconciliation of a particular point of view. My conscious parts were moved into a more appropriate alignment in order to receive and understand the direct experience that was to follow.

These infusions of conceptual clarity ran alongside of the speaking, weaving a web secure enough to hold the shifts in consciousness that occurred. The intelligence behind the orchestration and delivery of appropriate experience always caught my attention and required me to recreate my understanding of how things worked. There was magic in the air and it was happening in me, through me and around me.

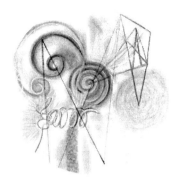

CHAPTER 5

COOPERATION

At the same time that the current opened me up to new views, I felt the impulse to reconnect with my earlier experience of working with clay. I discovered a wonderful art center upcountry on the island, and decided to attend a class in throwing on the potter's wheel. I came home from my first class in the late afternoon, tired and frustrated like any beginner learning a new skill. I walked into the house and found the walls of the living room covered with incredible drawings, abstract in nature and alive with energy.

Ellen was sitting on the couch with a beatific smile on her face. " I've been busy since you left," she informed me. With a sense of awe in my voice I asked her what had been going on. She told me that she had been guided by an inner voice to look at nature in a new way. While looking at flowers and butterflies, she had been instructed by this inner source to sit down and begin drawing. These pastel drawings were the result. A whole new capacity for seeing and expressing herself had been awakened in her.

In the following morning's sitting, Ellen's experience was referred to as an example of a larger process we were engaged with. It began in this way:

"What you were experiencing was a different way of perceiving. It is an example of letting the inner senses lead and express themselves without the restrictions imposed by the outer senses. You consider your outer receptors to be your only organs of perception. Your inner self also has its organs of perception, which are appropriate to, and aligned with, the vibratory landscape it occupies. You have physical eyes with which to see physical objects. However, with your eyes closed, you still see. You call these images. You attribute them to imagination, imbue them with lightness and airiness, and thus, with insubstantiality. Yet they are real, and are the result of an organ of perception, just like the eyes. One perceptual organ you make real; the other you make unreal. You rely on the outer organ to give you truth; the inner one you consign to fantasy. You act out of the information you receive from outer sight; you deny and are suspicious of inner sight.

Can you see the prejudice you have developed as a result of your belief about and your use of these perceptual capacities? It is now time to bring forward into conscious awareness the knowledge and direct perception of self that these inner senses provide. These areas of your being, while existing in silence, wait patiently in the wings for you to give them life, just as they give you life from moment to moment. Perception grants beingness. Inherent in the nature of every individual exists the organs of perception which, when used and activated, give birth to a new and more expanded selfhood."

With this inner coaching, we felt encouraged to let go of maintaining a hard line between our inner subjective experience and the outer objective form it was taking. We began to live within a more harmonious continuum of consciousness of inner to outer, and outer to inner.

Each reality had its own particular characteristics, and we became clear on their differences and did not expect them to logically reflect one another. This was enormously freeing for me. Instead of thinking that I was responsible for getting my inner and outer worlds to match or make sense, I relaxed. It was the experiential equivalent of the conceptual move I talked about earlier, when we made the choice to let go of understanding before allowing experience to take place.

As the sittings progressed, we were encouraged to cooperate with the process unfolding in our subjective experience, as well as in its outward expression. At first I thought I knew what cooperation meant. I had read enough spiritual literature to understand that it meant surrender in some form. Don't resist, surrender to your experience, and let go of identity. While there was a touch of this going on, it really meant something much more profound.

"This is the time in human development when the conscious mind of man has developed to a place where it is willing and capable of participating in its own illumination. When we talk about the conscious evolution of consciousness, we are talking about your ordinary self becoming a more conscious participant in the process of creating what is experienced. What is of importance here is the willingness to desire and open to new configurations of being."

As I stated earlier, I was becoming more comfortable

with the speaking and the state of consciousness I was in while it took place. I was becoming more attuned and present to the experience that was being delivered along with the statements. It was a multidimensional focus, I was simultaneously aware of my thoughts, my emotional reactions, and the body sensations that were being elicited.

I sensed myself as a spacious, open field of awareness that embodied thoughts, feelings and sensations as objects belonging to the field itself.

When the above statements were made about cooperation and willingness, I saw how each level of experience had its place and part to play in the overall creation of my current state of being. Each level was safe to be itself and, at the same time, recognize itself as belonging to something larger. From this vantage point, I saw and understood what was meant by the conscious mind having arrived at a place where it could safely desire to know itself past its currently accepted boundaries. *The conscious mind had achieved the strength to look inward and outward simultaneously without being threatened by the loss of its own sense of place and its own sense of identity.*

Soon after I had this insight, the speaking addressed it. I was learning that what I took to be my subjective space was open and permeable and shared by the other layers of my larger self. This would often happen while the speaking experience was taking place; sometimes there was a comment, a train of thought, or a feeling I had in response to what was being expressed by the speaking. It was a direct example of what was under discussion. In other words, what I experienced at one level affected how the larger whole organized itself in response.

"There is a shift in emphasis now possible. Historically speaking, there has been an attempt to transcend or pass over the conscious self or ego, that part of your overall consciousness that is focused so intensely in physical reality. This attempt at transcendence has resulted in a picture and experience of man being separated from more elevated aspects of his own nature. It supports the view of man having fallen, or having been separated, from grace and now challenged to recapture his true nature. You have set yourselves the task of overcoming perceived obstacles as a way of developing heroic qualities and capacities that have strengthened the sense of a separate, physical self. This misunderstanding has been necessary to bring forth new experience.

In order to realize the whole, the time has come to join with the self instead of resisting and denying its parts. Understanding the profound cooperation that supports you into being will change your very perception of what and who you are. It will require that you expand your boundaries and accept your own experience as an expression of more than fate, capricious whim, or mechanical determinism."

After speaking the above material, I sat quietly for many minutes in a vast stillness. I felt my conscious mind trying to understand the implications of what was said by beginning to formulate a question. Before it could take shape the speaking responded with the following statement:

"Consciousness and the conscious mind are not synonymous. The conscious evolution of consciousness does not refer to the conscious mind altering itself by its own activity. It is a joint process whereby the inner self presents new material to the mind and, by this presentation, the mind explores new possibilities for itself. It is a cooperative and creative effort. Perceptual integration is the means of this evolution."

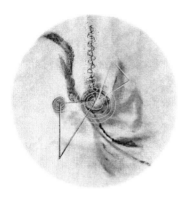

CHAPTER 6

THE IN-BETWEEN

I am standing in five feet of water about 50 yards off shore. Wearing my snorkel mask, I slowly submerge until I see half surface and half underwater. In this moment, I am on the cusp of a split view of my physical reality. With just a slight shift in attention, I belong to the surface of things and with another shift I belong to the depths. I am experiencing two different worlds, each containing the landscape and life appropriate to the medium it represents. Each world appears separate from the other as I hold the water line through the center of my mask. Yet I know they belong to a larger whole, with each contributing and cooperating with the other to produce the physical environment I know.

This split view while snorkeling was a perfect metaphor for how we were living our daily life at this time. Ellen and I now sat twice a day, in the early mornings and at dusk when the light began to leave the island. After morning sitting, we rode on the residue of this energy for the rest of the day. We dove into the beauty of Maui, either looking for good snorkeling beaches, or discovering new hiking trails and waterfalls. In one moment we were outside of time and space, embedded in a multidimensional focus, and in the next moment, we were enjoying the sequence of linear events in ordinary time.

"You are normally related to a self to whom you give substantial form. Viewed from the outside, using your physical senses, you seem substantial and solid to yourself. Like all other objects in your perceptual field, you appear to occupy space and demonstrate mass. As you can appreciate in this moment, the perception of space and volume is a product of the perceiver, not the object of perception itself."

A few minutes before this statement was made in sitting, I had experienced a strange sense of being elongated, like a rubber band being stretched. Using a physical metric, I felt like I was twenty or thirty feet tall. This was very different than the spaciousness I usually felt while the speaking was taking place. In checking with Ellen after the sitting, she had also experienced a change in size and shape.

"Once you begin to journey inside your experience, space can appear differently. You begin to sense that the Self enjoys many different qualities of space and form. Your outer view delivers up a self that is substantial and fixed. Your inner experience gives you a self that is more open, malleable and subject to change in form. In this sense, you are full and empty simultaneously. This illustrates your multidimensional nature; you are form and solid, and yet not."

As this statement ended, my size changed back to the round, spacious field I normally experienced while speaking. My attention was then drawn down and into sensations associated with my physical body. I use the word associated, because the body did not feel solid. Instead, it felt like a moving, flowing sensory field of energy. Only when I opened my eyes and looked at the body from the outside did I become solid to myself, and take on the characteristics of objective reality.

Just when I was getting clear about the inside and outside being different yet valid, this statement was introduced in the following sitting:

"As you awaken more subtle senses, you will begin to see there are many forms that will emerge within your experience. These forms will, in fact, transcend the experience of insideness. Inside is used here to give and point to a direction of attention or focus. In reality, inside is simply a device, one of the many possible qualities of focus available within consciousness; it is a point of view. We wish to recognize the experience of inside for its alignment as a doorway to walk through; we do not wish you to overly identify yourself with it."

The speaking continued to clarify why subjective experience was emphasized over outer perception. The most intimate movement of thought, feeling and sensation can be observed and experienced at this point of self-awareness—our inner subjectivity. More subtle relationships can be discerned here before our outer behavior begins to carry them away from their source of origin.

Of course, it is within ourselves that we also often feel the most confusion and lack of power. Our outer world appears more open and susceptible to being moved by an act of will through action. I can get up from sitting and walk around the room. I can ask a friend to join me for lunch, and he will show up across the table from me. I can move objects and create circumstances and influence the unfolding of events.

However, within our own experience of self, we may feel most at odds with the movements that occur, whether in thought, feeling, or sensation. It appears harder to change a negative thought pattern than to walk around the room, harder to control reactive feelings than to ask a friend to lunch, and harder still to manage uncomfortable sensations, like anxiety, than to throw a party. Our seeming lack of conscious control over these movements leaves us at the effect of our most intimate sense of self.

Despite this, Ellen and I were encouraged to view subjective self-experience as the most productive location to explore. At the same time, we were supported in accepting the changes that occurred as a consequence of this exploration.

"As the process you are engaged in unfolds, your perceptions will become more refined. You are now in the process of vibratory shifts. These shifts bring new qualities of perception within your own system, as well as between your system and other energy systems. Treat these new shifts with care and attention by validating your own experience without the need to label or intellectualize. New energies are present within your system. They will affect you like someone beginning to play a musical instrument; you must become familiar with the sounds and the notes that comprise the music your instrument produces. You are developing the sensitivity that quite naturally exists at these vibratory rates."

A couple of days later, after receiving the above transmission, Ellen and I were sitting in a restaurant having lunch. During a break in our conversation, I began to stare out the window next to me. I saw two birds who appeared to be dancing and playing with each other. As I looked more closely, I saw one bird scratching the earth below its feet while the other walked back and forth in front of the scratcher. Apparently something irresistible was uncovered by the scratching of the first bird, because the second bird moved in quickly, bent down and swallowed whatever had been exposed. I thought, "That's cute—survival of the fittest; the more aggressive bird gets the worm."

What happened next, however, began to initiate the current I described in Chapter 2. Now the birds reversed roles. Bird two began scratching while the first bird waited to be reciprocated for its previous effort. Sure enough, bird two started dancing and scratching, turned up something that bird one quickly moved in and consumed. I was amazed at how they were cooperating with each other. Right after that observation, I began to experience an infusion of energy coursing through me, and felt myself entering the state I normally enjoyed during the speaking. Subjectively, I felt very large, round and spacious, yet empty and insubstantial at the same time. As I looked out from this space, I saw that, objectively, I was sitting in a very public space with many people and objects surrounding me. Everything became still while in my head I had an epiphany that reconciled my confusion about what it meant to be present in time and space, yet also be outside of their constraints as well.

While holding both experiences together, I saw the source of my confusion. I had been trying to understand and reconcile their differences with my conscious mind. I was using a tool, designed to comprehend a dualistic reality, to understand a non-dual reality. The mind cannot hold time and space together with a reality beyond time and space. Only direct experience can accomplish this. In other words, one has to directly experience a multidimensional focus before the mind can create a concept to represent it. To begin to understand our true nature is to experience the profound cooperation necessary for them to exist as inner and outer realities.

The experience in the restaurant was an attempt to upgrade and inform my conscious mind so that it was in alignment with, and represented, my direct experience. I was being shown that the inside and the outside exist simultaneously and cooperatively – what I later understood as a perceptual integration. The next morning the speaking addressed my restaurant experience:

"The conscious mind remains active as this process of expansion takes place, and accesses and creates pictures of what is beyond itself. There is a choice that can be made here. It is the ability of the conscious mind to willingly fall back into itself and make room for a larger process. When you begin to have these moments of experience where time and space are different than you normally know them to be, accept them quickly. Time and space are the first perceptual constructions to be affected, and can serve as clues to the presence of a more inclusive experience. Choose to support the possibilities that they represent. Clarity will be achieved by allowing the confusion to live until it is no longer needed as a bridge of transition.

Confusion, while it is contrary to your experience, is an opening for the emergence of the new. There are elements of your experience which are perplexing and confusing and that seem to remove the stability and constancy you believe you seek. If you include these experiences as belonging naturally to your own process, you will begin to experience the contribution and the source of learning that is their purpose. The internal landscape is there for you to realize yourself. The external landscape is there for you to actualize yourself. They work hand in hand, each offering the other its completion. While they appear separate in your experience, their union is a complete one."

CHAPTER 7

CREATIVITY

The more playful and comfortable we became with the unexpected, the more we experienced an extraordinary outpouring of creative energy. The process included dreams, paintings, working with clay, meditation, and inspired infusions when the current would take us into multidimensional moments of expanded awareness.

Deep inner resources were being released and bubbling to the surface, ready to be experienced and integrated with the ordinary self and a more expanded state of being. We were learning about the cooperative nature of consciousness in action and becoming a conscious partner in the process.

Ellen wrote the following about her experience: "I was now engaged full time in new and deeper experience. My dream state and my waking state were both alive with geometric form, energetic out-picturing and teaching. When

Gary and I were not sitting together, I was following inner instructions on receiving light, allowing my vibration to be raised, transmitting energetic pictures on paper, and letting go to a spaciousness of being that I had never before experienced. I often had days to myself since Gary had felt the impulse to begin working with clay again. He would come home after many hours at the art center and walk into a house full of drawings and pictures and just shake his head in wonder. I was having the same experience I had witnessed when he was creating his clay heads. I was watching an inner capacity, full and mature, emerge out of nowhere."

In our sittings, we were being talked to about the process of natural perception. Pre-existing structures, consisting of conceptual beliefs and past conditioning, tend to confirm or select out perceptions, which are appropriate and meaningful to a person. There is a constant stream of perceptual information, which is either accepted, or not accepted, into conscious awareness, depending upon whether the information is recognized as familiar to the conscious self. This selection process takes place with such speed and cooperation from elements of our consciousness, which lie below our everyday awareness, that the process goes unobserved by the conscious self. The result is that we perceive with consistency and therefore, live in a world that gives back to us a sense of regularity and stability.

Our everyday conscious self is committed to seeking satisfaction within the structures and meaning already known to it. This part of the self seeks the familiar, strives for constancy and expects experience to reflect its conception of normal, however individually this is held. This is the realm of the outer self. Its job is to organize, process and manage our connection with the world and our place within it, a necessary and important function while embodied in form.

When Ellen and I made the choice to open ourselves to new and novel experience, this intention was transmitted throughout these cooperative elements of self, and initiated an environment that supported a new configuration for perceiving. A new foundation was established to receive fresh perceptions which otherwise would have gone undetected and unrecognized within our normal experience. The speaking confirmed that this expanded reality had resulted from our desire and intention to open and expand.

One morning in sitting, Ellen heard an inner voice, which told her that she would be receiving further inner teaching about her artwork. She was asked to do a drawing and was given some brief instructions as to shape and color. As she completed the drawing and set it aside, the question came into her mind, "Can I call you something?" She then saw pictures in her mind and heard the statement, "Klee is here and will teach you now." Her hand moved boldly over the paper and wrote the name Klee. The name was not familiar to her.

The following day, we drove into town to do some shopping. On impulse we went to a bookstore and started looking at books on the history of art. We came across the name Paul Klee, a famous abstract artist of the early 20th century. We couldn't believe it. What a wonderful confirmation in the world for the inner process we were engaged in. Klee was described as bringing in new inner harmonies as part of the Bauhaus School, a new movement in art at the time that was attempting to shake off old beliefs and create new forms. He said of himself that he had one foot in the physical world and one foot in the spiritual world.

As if this was not enough evidence for the continuity and synchronicity between our inner and outer realities, more evidence knocked on our front door two days later. A neighbor was dropping by to let us know that it was okay for us to pick and eat the papayas that grew along the property line between the two houses. Not having been introduced since we had moved into the house many weeks before, we invited him in. No one could enter the house at this time without noticing all of Ellen's drawings covering the walls. As we chatted, he scanned the walls and then walked directly up to the drawing she had done days before in sitting. He paused in front of it for a moment and then said, "Gee ... that looks just like a Paul Klee." We were shocked and quickly just nodded. A few minutes later he left. We stood there transfixed, both grinning at each other. It felt like we had just experienced a visitor from another dimension, whose sole purpose was to materialize at our front door, walk in and give testimony, and walk out, never to be seen again.

In our evening sitting the speaking again reiterated the concept of a unified field of experience.

"You will begin to see that, as you relate to your own experience as cooperative in nature, the world outside will also begin to act in accordance with this perception. You cannot have an event take place within private perception and not have a corresponding change in your external affairs. Again, these are not fundamentally two separate domains, but simply two faces belonging to the same perceptual field. You experience them as private and public, but that is only how you have organized and chosen to experience your world."

We were encouraged to accept that our growth would not appear as linear, but rather as random and unexpected, with no pattern that the conscious mind could repeat or duplicate purposefully at this time. We were engaged in a multidimensional form of learning that required participation of many levels of consciousness. Each level was open and receptive to a constant exchange of influence. I call this exchange between levels of consciousness *dynamic reciprocity*. Many levels of self were being affected by the experience we were having; this was a group effort involved in a creative act of consciousness.

From a more comprehensive point of view, the learning process exhibited the most profound intelligence and wisdom. It was quite natural for us to expect a logical, linear and sequential learning curve, because that was how our experience was usually organized and primed to produce. However, we were being given the opportunity to experience learning and living from a more multi-layered and multi-faceted vantage point, one that encompassed a greater appreciation for the marvelous, unexpected and sudden steps in our own growth.

"Life is creative, not mechanical. We are attempting to aid you in moving into a level of consciousness that acknowledges this creative dynamic within its own nature, that appreciates its ongoing movement towards fulfillment and illumination, and that enjoys the vitality and excitement of being engaged in a creative action within being."

51

As the weeks rolled by, we slipped in and out of linear time and space, filling many notebooks with the wisdom and coaching that issued from our morning and evening sessions.

"There is a shift now taking place within man's relationship to consciousness. The emphasis is on uniting and developing new boundaries in being that contain within them cooperative relationships that unify the Self, and generate new patterns of creativity. The point is to create not only an inner harmony, but also a new recognition of the contribution of all parts of your nature in the expression of life. There is nothing that you are a part of, or is a part of you, that is extraneous or does not contribute, through its own aliveness, to the well being of what you are. If humans can unite as a family and join together in their common task of being in the world, then it is time to turn within your experience and embrace the support and resources that your family in consciousness can provide."

One morning as we settled ourselves into our sitting, expecting our familiar experience to occur, there was silence. I experienced the same elevation in state but without the impulse to speak. This was true for the days that followed. We began to understand that things were going to change.

Except for brief visits from our three sons and some close friends, we had only related to each other for many months. We knew this had been necessary in order to support and generate the experience we were having. We started feeling that it was time to bring our new level of consciousness back into an everyday life that was not so isolated or secluded. We had opened and nurtured a connection with a deeper source of inspiration and wisdom, and it was time to find out if this new relationship could be maintained and serve as a support and resource within normal everyday living. We decided to leave the island.

We had arrived in Maui with the intention of giving ourselves the experience of no future. We wanted to wake up each day, free of any structures or expectations that were not part of the present we were generating. We wanted to renew our relationship with one another, and deepen our bond as we moved into the second half of our lives together. We also wanted to follow up on Ellen's commitment to explore the source of the voice that spoke to her while critically ill, which had suggested to her that her future was tied to finding the quiet within herself. We had been wonderfully successful with all three.

What we didn't know, and couldn't have known, was that these intentions belonged to the surface of a much deeper action that would emerge and catapult us into a whole new shift in consciousness. We were looking for renewal; what we received was a *perceptual integration*, a transformation in being. Because our experience was so dramatic and direct, we were left with the task of making sense of it. We had to let our minds catch up with the action, formulate new ideas and beliefs, and use these to fuel further creative engagement with our new state of being.

To give ourselves the time and space to accomplish this task, we decided that living a more rural life style would best support our needs. Within a few weeks, we were off the island and back on the mainland looking for a place to relocate. We spent time exploring the Taos and Santa Fe areas of New Mexico and parts of Colorado. While staying in a small cabin perched atop a ridge overlooking one of the old mining towns near Boulder, Colorado, it became clear to us that we needed to return to where we had started, California.

The truth is, we had loved the life we left in California. We had not left it out of dissatisfaction. If we were to continue our exploration and learn how to cultivate this new state within everyday life, what better place to do it than among family, friends and the life of service that characterized the work we did for a living. We had discovered ourselves in receiving; we now wanted to complete ourselves by giving.

CHAPTER 8

MAKING SENSE

To have so many aspects and dimensions of self-experience converge and cooperate to create a shift in consciousness leaves one's conscious mind in awe and wonder, especially when most of the action falls outside of its purview and control. Ellen and I had been continually encouraged to let the mind step aside so that other parts of the self could step forward and contribute without interference from a heavily saturated rational point of view. In other words, we were asked to suspend judgment until the results were in. In choosing this stance, a space was created for direct experience to lead; we had to trust that our minds were partners in the process, and would contribute appropriately when their qualities served to support the whole. Not an easy thing to do, given that each one of us has a personal identity grounded in the belief that what can't be physically seen or controlled is dangerous, and is therefore a threat to its survival. How to make sense of our Hawaiian experience?

The speaking itself provided the clues. It had stated that we were engaged in the conscious evolution of consciousness, and that the conscious mind was now able to participate in its own illumination. What did this mean?

The statement referred to the possibility that rational thought or cognition is not the seat of the self, but instead only a part of a larger whole. We human beings, especially in the West, have identified our essential selves as resting within the stream of narrative voices we hear in our heads. We have collapsed our essential identity down to this one aspect of self-experience. We have each reduced the self to its own conception of itself.

The truth is, however, that we are not our thoughts. We *have* thoughts. In making this distinction, we make it possible to separate thought from self-awareness. Thinking about yourself is different than being aware of yourself. When this distinction is made clear, it makes room for other aspects of self to share the light that attention can shine on the moment of perception, and perhaps give new direction to our search for who and what we are.

When we make this shift from we are our thoughts to we have thought, the mind is released from the burden of being the carrier of personal identity. The mind can now imagine beyond its own boundaries without losing its ground of being.

It can see its own limitations. Knowing what it doesn't know and can't know by using itself as the source, the mind becomes a partner in the process of growth and evolution.

It can relinquish its control and is free to receive and entertain new material though intuition, imagination, inspiration and revelation.

The speaking stated that the method to facilitate ones conscious evolution was the process of *Perceptual Integration*. What is this action or dynamic? Let's examine the word perception first. The moment of perception is made up of two components. The first is conceptual. The second is sensory experience. They make up the mind/ body field we inhabit. The mind holds the idea, and the body uses its five senses to translate the concept into a meaningful and recognizable form. Only when we have the concept chair can we organize the sensory form necessary to see it and sit in it. Without the idea and the sensory apparatus to perceive its form and substance, we have no objective perception of chair.

The speaking kept falling on the side of consciousness being first, with physical reality following in reference to the act of knowing or perceiving. This point of view established the context for the experiences I encountered with the current or infusions of insight described in Chapter 3. The movement and source of creative action is subjective to objective, from inside to outside, both playing their cooperative roles in forming a perceptual loop and a natural learning environment in which to grow, expand and evolve.

I create or accept an idea. This idea is then translated into a physical form so that I can encounter it in experience, and thus know the nature of my creation. This feedback allows me to meet myself in action, and provides the material I need on a conscious level to continue to reinvent my experience and my ideas. It points me in the direction of generating a more unified field between my inner and outer realities.

Here is an example of uncovering this dynamic while infused with the current.

I am attempting to recognize that my world is my creation. In the past, I tried to maintain stability between my inner experience and my outside reality in an attempt to resolve the experience of separation I feel. I now see that only by taking responsibility for creating my beliefs as my own creation, can I move into the position of transforming this separation. I need to embrace what I perceive to be true so I can see what I have created.

My beliefs have to become perceivable (experienced) in order to be seen and owned as mine. If my beliefs aren't made real or manifest, they build on each other. I go from idea to idea without any validation that justifies them as being true in experience.

It is important to start making my beliefs more accurately reflect my direct experience, instead of trying to make my experience match my beliefs. Perceptual integration occurs when my beliefs and my experience become aligned with each other. From this integration, a sense of grace and ease occurs that grants permission to continue to create.

Here is a mundane example from my experience that illustrates this principle in operation. A number of years ago, friends asked Ellen and I to dinner. They suggested Japanese food. I told them I don't like Japanese food. After some persuasion, off we went to their favorite Japanese restaurant. The food was delicious and I loved it. A few months passed by and different friends asked us to dinner. Japanese food was brought up as a possibility. I immediately stated that I don't like Japanese food, and asked if we could pick something else. Ellen reminded me that the last time I had Japanese food I loved it. I started to resist her information and defend my belief when I remembered my experience of actually eating it. Guess what! I loved it again.

I don't even know where the belief that I didn't like Japanese food came from. I grew up in a family from the Midwest and dinner for us was meat, potatoes and vegetables out of a can. There was never any foreign food eaten. I had been given, or developed, a belief that I had resisted putting to the test of direct experience. Instead, I went from idea to idea with no intervening direct experience to justify it as a legitimate guideline for action.

What is my point here? If each of us looks at those deeper and more profound beliefs about reality that have no direct experience to support them, we can begin to see how we have diminished, by belief alone, the possibility for a greater perception of what is real. The speaking conveyed this over and over again and demonstrated it by delivering a multilayered direct experience that generated new ideas and beliefs to be integrated and used for further creation. In the second part of this book, I go deeper into this part of the Perceptual Integration process so the reader can follow along and use it to develop a more integrated state of being.

Let's look at the second half of the term Perceptual Integration. What is meant by integration? In the dictionary, the word is defined as the act or instance of combining into a unified whole, or pertaining to or belonging as part of the whole. In my experience, this is the part of the process that was hard to observe in action. When it comes to change or growth in ourselves, we have a hard time accounting for how we arrived at where we are. We walk through the front door of ourselves as if entering a room and then leave through the back door, but we have little memory of what took place in the room itself. The change in our behavior can be plotted, but a change in thought, feeling, attitude or point of view is harder to account for. Subtle shifts in consciousness or state of being are even more difficult to see.

During our time in Hawaii I became aware of an intelligent pattern, operating throughout the action of integration, which instilled in me a profound trust in the wisdom inherent in our nature as consciousness. The first step of this pattern was to separate the parts of the self. Once the separate parts were distinguished and held in awareness, the resulting space could be used to organize a new set of relationships and a new state of being.

We have all experienced this reorganization as part of the natural process of growing and maturing. The baby becomes the child through a series of learning imperatives it must master in order to move on to the next stage of development. He or she must first encounter the limitations of its current state in order to move on to the next step. To stand, crawl, walk, or speak requires that old distinctions be integrated and new ones adopted. This continues though life, old age, death and after. We fall apart and are put back together again into a new configuration that allows for continued growth.

Throughout the whole speaking experience, I was shown the differences between the parts that made up the conscious self I knew, and their relationship to the larger, more refined state of consciousness to which they belonged. I didn't know it at the time, but after the speaking stopped and we left the island, I took the speaker with me. The split between the speaker and the self I knew had integrated and become one. I knew this was true because I continued to receive revelatory material as part of my normal everyday experience. Through some mysterious energetic, I had internalized the speaker. It now lived within me as a constant source of inspiration and wisdom.

When I returned to my family and friends on the mainland and was asked about my experience, my superficial answer was, I became smarter. This, of course, was not true. If you gave me an I.Q. test before and after our experience in Maui there would probably be no difference. Although I was no smarter, I *was* unaccountably deeper and richer in self-wisdom. It was as if a new template for processing experience had been instilled in me. It offered a more complex and graceful reality, one that was open and creative in nature and multidimensional in perception. *I was enjoying a more expanded self-awareness.*

PART TWO

BECOMING
SELF-AWARE

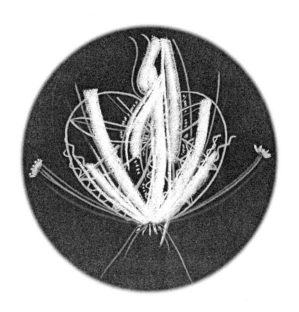

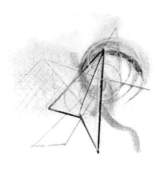

CHAPTER 9

LEARNING ABOUT YOUR SELF FROM YOURSELF

SHAPE IT OR IT WILL SHAPE YOU

As an aspect of our experience self-awareness eludes easy definition. The Random House Dictionary gives us only the words 'self' and 'awareness', leaving us to forge a meaningful melding of the two on our own. For our purposes, we can define the concept of self-awareness as having conscious experience of one's subjective experience. This gives us a place to begin and allows us to become knowledgeable about the mechanics that underlie our subjective life.

Self-awareness is much easier to recognize when someone demonstrates its presence. We can see and intuit that there is an ephemeral quality or capacity behind the thoughts, feelings or behavior being expressed. It is implied and informs their action while never being seen. I remember watching an interview between an intelligent, highly respected American journalist and the Dalai Lama. The journalist asked him what was the most important thing anyone could do to bring happiness and grace to their life. Without hesitating, he replied, "Cultivate self-awareness."

Not moments after this exchange, I watched the most extraordinary demonstration take place. While they continued to talk, a fly began buzzing between them. The journalist reflexively reached out to catch and kill it with his hand. He missed, and his action moved the fly into the Dalai Lama's space. Just as reflexively as the journalist, the Dalai Lama slowly raised his arm, and with a gentle pushing movement, escorted the fly out and away.

This moment perfectly illustrated two different ways in which self-awareness can be organized. It can be built from the outside in, or from the inside out. Both are legitimate, but have different consequences. The Western journalist had reduced his self-awareness to the boundary between his physical body and the world. Thus the fly was other, and an irritation to be done away with. For the Dalai Lama, self-awareness had been a lifelong practice built from the inside out. The result was a more inclusive awareness, one that didn't stop at the boundaries of his body, but included a larger energetic space that recognized his connection to the world.

Each of the above examples demonstrates the capacity for self-awareness to either contract or expand, resulting in different configurations in being. We can see that our capacity for self-awareness is an open system, subject to the cultural and personal experiences of its carrier. While we are all endowed with this capacity for self-awareness, it is what we do with it that determines the shape it takes and the reality we encounter.

If we are to consciously explore becoming self-aware, it is important to remind ourselves that our beliefs are working models about the nature of reality. Our beliefs are conceptual devices for manufacturing structure and meaning; they are not attributes of the self that need to be protected and justified by misperception and denial of direct experience. Our beliefs are an ever changing mosaic that we encounter and experience as part of a creative projection of self. We are granted the freedom to invent, imagine, experiment and play in a way that is not possible if we hold these working models to be inviolate and belonging to our very essence. To explore consciousness while being engaged in daily life, it is necessary to envision our lives as the field of play in which we can generate the experience we wish to support into being.

WHERE IS THE WORLD?

My ongoing experience with multidimensional realities has given me evidence that we don't exist in the world. Instead the world exists within us. The world we know as real, solid and physical is a product of a creative act of perception, whose genesis lies beyond its outward manifestation. Our five outer senses (sight, taste, touch, smell and hearing) allow us to receive and navigate in the world. Yet equally important inner senses exist which precede these outer senses.

To explore whether the world exists within or outside

of *us* is an exercise in examining direct experience. And if we only look to confirm the ideas or concepts produced by the conscious mind, we may miss the opportunity to go beyond ordinary reality where new concepts, and therefore new experiences, can be realized.

In truth, there is a much deeper creative process at work than we are usually aware of. In order to play, we need a playing field that is open and flexible, into which we enter as powerful players—a field in which the world and the self live as an act of perception.

Travelling into expanded states of consciousness always leaves me amazed at the inherent spontaneity and creative play that characterizes higher levels of consciousness. This re-envisioning of ordinary reality is necessary if we are to shift our attitude from one of serious work to one of playful self-exploration; and if we are to end the struggle between striving and resistance, aspiration and resignation. The intention is not to challenge the ordinary self to become something it is not, but to see through it to a self that is already enjoying its own grace. We want to maintain this playful attitude so that we can continue to be receptive and open to further contact and inspiration from the self we seek to bring into awareness.

The starting place in becoming self-aware is our inner state of being in the moment. To understand what I mean by *state of being*, imagine a soap bubble around your physical body.

The inside of the bubble represents your subjective world, filled with all the thoughts of the mind, feelings and sensations of the body and the energetic subtleties that belong to the *field of energy and awareness* that surrounds the mind/body.

This is your subjective world, and any perceived moment of its unfolding represents your state of being. The physical forms we perceive with our five senses fall outside of the bubble and represent your outer world, the world of material objects.

When our attention is grounded in the here and now, recognizing emerging experience as perceptual in nature, we have established what the speaking called our *point of perception*. From this point of perception we can look out into our physical world or look into our inner world with grace and ease. From this vantage point within our subjectivity, we can enter into play with our unfolding experience and become a conscious partner in its creation.

SEPARATING THE PARTS

Deepening our self-awareness necessitates separating out the aspects of self-experience so that they can be clearly differentiated and held in awareness. Once separated and recognized as discrete parts, something magical happens. The parts start to rearrange themselves and fall into a new alignment that produces greater self-awareness, and makes these parts more available to conscious control.

A good example of this is how we experience anger. We typically become angry in response to a perceived threat. We attempt to feel powerful in the face of feeling vulnerable. The thought, *I am being threatened* and the feeling of power we need to confront that thought arrive so quickly, one right after the other, that we often do not know which aspect we are experiencing, and simply accept the resulting gestalt as a whole in itself. What results is a defensive posture where thought and feeling are used together to justify the particular behavior that follows.

When this happens, it obscures the dynamic relationship that exists between these two parts, thought and feeling, and often results in diminished awareness and loss of conscious control. We become disempowered and eventually we feel victimized by our thoughts and feelings, with no say in their impact on our state of being in the moment. The separation of these parts of our self allows us to see where we have collapsed two aspects and blurred their boundaries, accepting the two as one.

Here is an example. Ellen and I have an argument and I say to her, "I don't think you love me." She, listening carefully, says back to me, "Do you think I don't love you or do you feel like I don't love you?" I've collapsed thinking and feeling and have given her a confused message. Once I am aware of this lack of distinction, I can then respond, "I think you love me, but I just feel like you don't right now." Now the conversation can take a more constructive direction than it might have because we are clear about what we are addressing. In our communications with one another, these collapsed distinctions can create much confusion and suffering. It also places the burden of making these distinctions on our listener's shoulders rather than looking at our selves as the source.

This dynamic is also true at the multidimensional level. Often in the midst of expanded perception, we confuse the sight and knowledge available at a higher level of consciousness with our everyday consciousness, as though experiencing something on a more refined level means it can be retained by our ordinary consciousness. Instead of expanding our identity to include the many levels and layers that make up a more comprehensive self, we attempt to collapse it all into the smaller, more familiar container of the ordinary self. It can be disappointing when, back in our normal state, we cannot remember the knowledge or retain the point of view that was so natural to the elevated state, or replicate the form and substance that characterize the self at this higher level.

An expanded state of consciousness is more open and fluid and can move and join with any object held in it's perception; all boundaries are open and porous. Only when a perceptual integration occurs, when a resonance exists between two levels of consciousness, does the denser level of our physical being begin to be transformed and take on the qualities of the higher state. This is how the conscious self grows and evolves.

For example, in the speaking experience I collapsed two different levels of consciousness.

When I would return to my normal consciousness after sitting, I would be confused that I couldn't retain the sense of expansion I enjoyed while in the speaking space. I would naturally take on the form and density of my normal state. I expected my normal state to be transformed into the larger simply by contact or having experienced qualities belonging to its frequency.

Only after repeating the shift from my normal everyday state of consciousness to the more expanded state I enjoyed while speaking did I begin to recognize them as separate and complete, each enjoying their place within a more comprehensive self-experience. My conception and experience of self became larger because each state was accepted and distinct. The smaller self did not become the larger self. Instead, my awareness expanded to include more dimensionality then I was previously conscious of. I was simply more than I thought I was. Just like when we separate thought and feeling from one another, each becomes more available to experience fully and to be used creatively to construct our state of being in the moment.

CHAPTER 10

THE THREE SKILLS

THE NEED

After returning to Palo Alto from Hawaii, I began re-establishing my private practice in psychotherapy. Old clients returned and new referrals began to increase, and it wasn't long before I was back working a full schedule of appointments. This was important to me. I have always loved the exchange of intimacy and energy that takes place in sessions and feel privileged to be allowed into another person's experience and world. What added to this pleasure was the new state of consciousness I now brought to these encounters. While listening deeply to a client, I found myself slipping into a state of expanded perception similar to the state I enjoyed while sitting in meditation and receiving the speaking experience.

I became very still and sensed expanding boundaries in all directions until a feeling of quiet presence pervaded the space between my client and me. This space listened and received what the client was presenting differently than I did in my normal everyday state. No judgment or interpretation intruded into the space between us. The client's experience was not filtered through any template of understanding on my part. I could see how they organized themselves into being in that moment.

After sitting with hundreds of people in this new state of consciousness, I began to see, that underlying our confusion and distress was always the *capacity* for self-awareness, but not the exercise of it. This was understandable. We have not been educated about the skills and knowledge necessary to live within our own skins or how to manage our subjective world. Growing up, all of our instructions are about how to be in the world, not how to be in ourselves. We are trained to be an object in an objective world, and encouraged to perfect the outer attributes of our personhood, our appearance and our behavior, instead of embracing the being that resides at the center of our experience.

Working with others, I arrived at the same conclusion I had come to regarding myself, i.e., that there was a need to learn how to become self-aware and develop skills for managing one's state of being in the moment. A method was needed that was not therapeutic (assuming that something was psychologically wrong), or religiously based, (assuming that some form of redemption was necessary), but instead *educational;* a method that could be used to organize ourselves into a more graceful state of being and allow us to bring skillful self-awareness to the issues we encounter in our lives.

Since I was experiencing this in a very palpable way, I needed to learn this for myself. I also understood that it was a universal need, given the fact that, in order to solve the issues facing the world as a whole, our state of consciousness would have to change and evolve.

What better way to support this than to practice it and achieve some mastery so I could share it with others?

I have written this book in a way that casts me in the role of the student in hopes that by sharing my experience it will inspire and illuminate your learning as well. Embedded in my experience is the condensed experience of the thousands of students who have used the methods outlined in this book.

There are three basic skills that embody becoming self-aware that lead to living within your self with skill and grace. These three skills are:

1. Taking control of your attention.

2. Grounding your self in the fact of the body.

3. Releasing your self from the fiction of the mind.

These three skills will help us establish the point of perception, a location within our experience that establishes the platform and center from which to explore and expose the self in operation. Taken together, these three skills will launch you on a personal journey that will lead to remarkable discoveries about your nature and your identity as a multi-layered being. Using the powerful capacity of attention to locate your point of perception, you will then be in position to discover and explore the subtle energy fields that are available through the *fact of the body*. You will then stabilize your presence at the point of perception by releasing yourself from *the fiction of the mind*. Each of these skills represents a shift in consciousness which, when practiced together, creates a platform from which to explore more deeply the mystery behind the appearance of the self we know.

CHAPTER 11

THE MAGICIAN AND HIS WAND

ATTENTION IS MAGIC

Even though it appears as if magic has disappeared from our modern world, in fact it still exists, and is very much alive. Magic lives within us in a form we rarely recognize, and therefore we have forgotten its use and function. The magic I am referring to is the role that *attention* plays in the construction of what we experience and how we perceive. When we begin to investigate the process of consciously taking control of our attention, we discover properties of attention that are truly magical.

Attention is the most powerful tool we have to work with. There is no other aspect of self-experience in which we have such direct control—not in our thoughts, feelings, sensations or behaviors. Our ability to focus and direct our attention at will, in the moment, is our most direct act of self-expression. Attention is the creative instrument we use to construct our state of being, and is the active dynamic that determines what we perceive at any given moment.

Imagine a symphony conductor standing on his podium in front of the orchestra he is directing. He and the musicians together are going to make music. As he stands, with his arms extended out and above his head, there is a baton in his right hand. He uses this baton to point to the musicians and the instruments he wishes to bring into the foreground, at the right time, and within the context of the piece being played. In our metaphor, the baton is attention and the conductor is the will that directs it. The magic that attention performs naturally as part of our everyday experience happens so smoothly, and with such congruency, that we barely notice its actions at all. We simply view its actions as normal and assign their miraculous properties to the mundane reality we inhabit. It wasn't until I investigated my own ordinary experience that I realized the extraordinary nature of attention.

Attention can travel across the barrier between subjective and objective reality without changing its form.

No other aspect of the self can do this. Attention can move from the world of matter, perceiving a material object, to the world of the mind, perceiving a thought, to the world of the body perceiving a sensation. It can also travel deeper into subjective reality and perceive energetic dimensions of higher consciousness, all without changing its nature—which is to focus, point, target and illuminate the object under its gaze.

Attention does this continuously, moving from our internal to our external perception of reality. There is no other aspect of self that can do this without first transforming and cloaking itself in the medium of the particular reality that it is showing up in. For example, thought resides in the mind until it crosses the barrier by becoming speech, written word or mimed through behavior. A feeling, which is subjective in nature, can only reside in the body; it has to remain as a felt experience until it is transformed into a public and objective act of self-expression.

You can verify this by simply sitting quietly, looking at an object near you. Look at the object and give it your complete attention. Then think about the object or any other thoughts or ideas running through your head in the moment. You have just shifted your attention across the barrier from an objective world to a subjective one.

Why is this important? Because our attention, the capacity to focus, point, target and illuminate a particular object of perception, can move throughout the whole spectrum of experience. It grants us access to the whole of self-experience, becoming our major tool for self-exploration.

Attention can join with any experience, no matter its substance or vibration.

Attention is always present regardless of the state of consciousness being experienced. It can target a thought, feeling, sensation or outer perceived object with ease. It can also point its conductor's baton toward and within higher states of consciousness, where the physical body no longer has substance, and the field of perception takes on more rarefied qualities. It is always where we are, regardless of the nature of identity at any level of being.

Attention always places us at the center of our experience.

As if tethered to an unseen force or presence, attention moves out and returns to the will that directs it. I never experience ordinary consciousness without the sense that my attention is in the service of me, the perceiver, instead of the object of my perception. Although attention reveals its object to the perceiver, it can keep the perceiver unknown to it self. *Only when attention is directed at the perceiver does the process of self-awareness begin.*

Attention can bring the movement of the moment to a standstill or it can join the stream of unfolding experience.

Attention has the ability to contract and expand. I can narrow and hold my focus on an object and stop the propensity of attention to keep moving. Or, I can allow my attention to follow the flow of movement from one moment to the next, illuminating and bringing into awareness new content.

Attention can expand to hold many different levels of experience simultaneously.

The term multidimensional implies a perceiver with a multilayered point of view, one where attention is active in discerning each layer and able to target experience within each layer. This capacity is central to meditation practice and is instrumental in allowing shifts in consciousness.

Attention can join with any inner or outer sense modality, and magnify its function.

Most of us have had the experience of listening to music while we stare off into space or float off into thoughts and pictures that the music evokes. In this common experience, attention moves between hearing, seeing and our inner sight. Each time it moves and lands on one of these modes of perception, it magnifies the experience, giving it more acuity and sharpness of focus. We are often moving from seeing, hearing, feeling, touching, smelling, thinking, sensing or imagining with such ease that, without being consciously focused on any one particular sense modality, we only experience a continuous stream of consciousness. Yet when we bring our full attention to any one of them, that particular experience jumps out and comes to the foreground; the other senses fall to the background with less sharpness and presence.

The ability of attention to determine the movement between foreground and background is important to cultivate and practice while learning to manage our state of being. This is because attention becomes a major tool for creating once we began to use it consciously. I will keep coming back to this powerful bit of magic throughout the book.

Attention can make things appear or disappear.

Here is an example in real time: Right now as I write these paragraphs, Ellen is using an automatic paper shredder, which is making a loud, grinding, electric whine just twenty feet behind me. The noise shifts to the background when I focus on the voice within me that is writing these sentences. When I stop writing, and shift my attention back into the room, the shredding sound becomes foreground. I can be so focused on my writing that the shredding sound actually disappears, only to reappear when my focus or concentration is broken. This shift in attention creates the movement between foreground and background that is so familiar to us.

The statement *"What you give your attention to, is"* embodies this particular magic. By focusing my attention, I can make things appear or disappear in the moment. I can be in thought one moment, then shift my focus and give my attention to the person sitting next to me. They can say something that pulls me back into thought, and then they disappear, replaced by an inner narrative, until I hear them asking for my attention again. This happens all the time as our attention moves and refocuses moment to moment.

We can even disappear and reappear the self we know. I am always amused when I discover that I have driven miles, without any awareness that I have done so, while lost in thought. I can't account for the distance or time I have traveled between two points of reference. We all have the experience of being so concentrated and focused in what we are doing that the activity replaces the self-consciousness we normally carry into each moment. The actor disappears into the action. We become one with the activity. We don't realize we have disappeared until we notice that our sense of being the perceiver has returned.

Attention can create time or timelessness.

This bit of magic is profound. Attention is instrumental in the creation of linear time. Without giving our attention to past or future thought projections, we find ourselves resting in the present moment. From this vantage point, time is a mental construct. This is extremely important as we learn to become more conscious with our use of attention. It leads to greater control over our state of being, particularly when it comes to how thoughts and feelings are processed and experienced.

The more we move into higher states and away from everyday consciousness, the sense of stepping out of time increases. *When attention is not being used by the conscious mind to create the conceptual categories of past, and future, there is a direct awareness of timelessness or eternal presence of the here and now.*

Attention is still present even when we are not.

Many of us have had some experience with this aspect of attention. For example, when we become awake in a dream, a lucid dream in which we are conscious that we are dreaming, we can follow the unfolding action with the same sense of attention that characterizes our normal awake state. Yet the usual self we know is unconscious and not present. This is just another example of the magic of attention. Whatever form we find ourselves in, attention seems to follow us; it is as if attention belongs to a more comprehensive awareness that includes all the manifestations we are capable of taking – a larger sense of self.

Another example of the phenomenon is an out of body experience. I have had several out of body experiences and in each one, the "I "apparently separate from the physical body was still able to direct attention and discern the particular details that constituted its point of view. For example, one evening Ellen was not feeling well, so we decided

I would sleep in the guest room, which was situated at the other end of the house. I had to walk down a hallway to a door that opened into the living room, which then gave me a view of the bedroom where Ellen was sleeping.

After retiring and starting to fall asleep, I suddenly jolted awake. In the moments just before coming into full consciousness, I found myself standing in the doorway in the hallway, looking through the living room and kitchen to the bedroom where Ellen slept. This lasted no more than a few seconds, enough time to consciously register the experience and ground myself in its sensory manifestation, before I was back in my body and woke up.

In those seconds, my field of perception was just as though the conscious part of me was standing there looking into Ellen's room. My attention was active, taking in all the cues and discernments as my view passed through the living room into the bedroom. Once back in my body and awake, my conscious mind could not account for being in two places at the same time. The two experiences had collapsed into one; I wasn't sure whether I had been dreaming the experience or not. However, future experiences left me with no doubt that I had in fact 'caught' myself outside the body, while still being able to perceive and direct attention.

Attention can be directed by choice or not.

This is one of the paradoxes of our being. It is this bit of magic that makes it necessary to practice taking control of one's attention. Our tendency to surrender to attention's automatic movement and conditioned preferences is a major source of our suffering. It throws us into reactive states of thought and feelings that dominate our ability to respond appropriately to the present.

While embodied, we inhabit a dual nature. Our physical wiring, coupled with the conscious mind's propensity toward pattern recognition, leaves us subject to the familiar, repetitive actions and decisions from the past. Relegated to the subconscious, these patterns of thought, feeling and perception free us from constant reassessment and create a continuity of experience. However, they also breed a separation from the authentic and accurate perception of the uniqueness of the moment.

In other words, when not consciously choosing our focus, it is chosen for us by habit and conditioning. Attention then serves our psychology, our habits of being and perception; it is used to satisfy us, not fulfill us.

Taking control of attention begins the essential process of breaking this unconscious habitual pattern. We start to regain the freedom to choose our focus, and therefore our perception, in the moment. We recognize attention as the major building block for creatively constructing our state of being.

All of the attributes of attention I have described in this chapter belong to the magic of normal everyday experience, and become the instrument used by the self, consciously or unconsciously, to create the reality we know and encounter. To practice the magic hidden within our capacity to focus and attend, we first have to become the conductor, practiced and comfortable with controlling where we point our baton.

CHAPTER 12

FINDING YOUR POINT
OF PERCEPTION

CHOOSING TO ATTEND

Like film, our outer senses provide a medium that records only the surface of our lives. We have learned to give most of our attention in this direction. What lies under the obvious is hidden from our view. Yet it is in plain sight if we choose to direct our attention there. However, our will to choose has been co-opted by habit in the service of our psychology. Our intention to be responsive and creative has been captured by our will to stay the same. As a way of gently intervening with this conditioned state, we must take the first step in developing our attention and returning it to our conscious control.

I started taking control of my attention by playing with the following experiment. Sitting in a chair, I focus my attention on every object I see as I move my sight around the room. I immediately notice that the object of my attention stands out and becomes foreground, taking on a sharpness and vividness in its appearance, while other objects recede and become less significant.

I then shift my attention to feeling my seat in the chair, my back against the back of the chair and my feet on the floor. If I am standing, I feel my feet on the ground. I go back and forth shifting my attention into the room and then shifting it back to a sensation in my body. Each shift is a conscious choice on my part to move the focus of my attention. Like a fly fisherman casting his line in front of him and then reeling it in, I cast my attention out into the world, the room, and reel it back in by feeling a sensation in my body. I go out and I come back in. This takes a split second and always reassures me that I am never far from myself, only a choice away.

With this simple shift of attention, I practice the magic that attention has for crossing the boundary between my internal and external reality and getting clear about where each is located. My five outer senses give me the perception of the room. If they were not active, the room would not exist for me. *Out there* is a creation that naturally occurs because I am built to perceive in this way. There is also a perception, belonging to some inside knowing, that is not a part of the outer senses, which produces the experience of *in here*, distinct and discrete from physical reality.

Having attention move from the inside to the outside and back to the inside is a natural movement that goes on constantly throughout the day. Most of the time it goes on automatically, without our conscious choice. When we do choose to focus during an activity we are engaged in, we may not be aware that we are choosing to do it, and thus relegate the choice to unconsciousness. Further, we may not be aware that we are crossing the line between two different realities. We take for granted the smooth transition that attention makes between the two states. By consciously practicing this shifting process until I could clearly distinguish these two halves of my experience, I became adept at shifting my attention at will between the two.

Then I began to practice this shift in attention in my daily activities. I had fun shifting from outside to inside! I walked into the market and gave my attention to my physical surroundings, taking in the sight and sounds, textures and smells on display. Then, as I walked down the aisles, I shifted between sensing my body pushing the cart and observing my feelings and thoughts. Or, sitting with a friend in conversation, I shifted between looking and listening to him and the feelings and thoughts that our conversation elicited in me, moving back and forth between the two experiences.

As this distinction became clear to me, I began to develop a natural awareness for noticing when my attention was moved outside and when it was moved inside, regardless of whether it was moved by the action of the moment or by conscious choice. I realized that when we distinguish the different parts that make up our experience, something happens that leads to greater self-awareness and integration. I began to experience an alignment that was clarifying and that deepened my ability to know my location in any moment of experience. I could start to differentiate between the experiences of here, inside, as compared to there, outside.

WHERE IS HERE?

It is often deeply confusing that our perception is split between "out there" and "in here." Our fundamental experience comes to us divided; where does the self end and the world begin? We apply a rather crude metric to make sense of it. We use private and public as a way of coming to terms with this confusion. What we perceive alone (sensation, thought and feeling) is labeled private and therefore subjective, belonging to the subject or perceiver. What is perceived as public can be seen and verified by others and is assigned as the object. Any behavior and action into the world belongs to the objective world. In daily life, any misunderstanding between subjective and objective experience sets the stage for high drama and suffering as we attempt to locate and manage our experience. When we are able to acknowledge and accept the distinction between inside and outside, the impact on our experience can run from simple to profound.

Here are some examples from everyday life. Ellen is sitting in her office and calls from the doorway, "Gary, where are you?" I am sitting in the living room and I answer, "I am here." With frustration in her voice she yells back, "Where is here?" When I recognize that my here is simply a location within my subjectivity and is not shared by Ellen, nor meaningful to her since she is sitting in another room and can't see me, I make the adjustment and call back, "I am here in the living room."

I am standing talking with a friend. He says to me, "The other night when we were talking to Mary, I didn't think you were very nice to her." I immediately feel hurt and judged. I assign the cause of my feelings to him and reply defensively "Well, that's because you're always trying to protect her." We are now in conflict. Without a clear distinction between out there and in here, we assign cause to the wrong location and suffer the consequences that naturally follow. My friend simply gave me his opinion, which belonged to him, out there. I took it in and manufactured my own response commensurate with its meaning for me. Not having a good grounding in my own here, I don't catch what I do, only what he does, and therefore I am left holding him as the cause of my feelings. If I had made a better distinction, I might have said, "That's interesting. How did you experience me?"

It is important to experience how we are separate from out there, the world, before we can properly know how we belong to it. This simple shift of attention from in here to out there and its corresponding distinctions begin to provide a sense of direction for locating ourselves in space, aiding us in finding the point of perception we seek.

A PERSONAL WORKING GEOGRAPHY

After playing with this distinction of inside and outside, I began to understand that what I was doing was generating a personal geography that could be used in a very practical way to make sense of my experience, as well as to generate more self-awareness. Not only was I practicing taking control of my attention and rescuing it from the tendency to move as dictated by old habits of conditioning, I was actually building a new template for constructing a more comprehensive state of being.

It *is* possible to be much more proactive in constructing our experience rather than living in a reactive and unconscious state. We don't have to be at the effect of ourselves. We can use the mechanics of experience in a creative way and become a conscious partner in the process—what the speaking experience referred to as *the cooperative nature of consciousness.*

This distinction between inside and outside is only the first step in our search. While it provides a new sense of location, this distinction alone is not enough to bring us to our point of perception where awareness of emerging experience can be distinguished. It is now necessary to move our focus more deeply to the inside of ourselves.

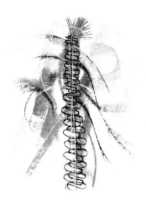

CHAPTER 13

THE UP AND DOWN

THINKING UP AND FEELING DOWN

began to see the shift of attention between inside and outside as a horizontal movement or the *horizontal axis of awareness*. Attention appeared to follow a straight horizontal plane, which connected the inside to the outside by using an invisible tether in my awareness. However, when I began to explore the inside more deeply, this geometry changed.

As I would sit and go inside, I observed my attention being caught in a vertical movement or *vertical axis of awareness*, between my thought process, and my feelings and bodily sensations—the mind and the body as experienced from the inside. When I found myself in thought, it was as if I was looking at pictures or hearing narratives in the space that my head occupies, right in front and slightly above the top of my forehead.

I have asked thousands of people where they receive and locate their experience of thinking, and all universally point to some location around the head. The common expression being in your head obviously confirms this observation.

The body of emotional feeling and sensation, however, always exists lower and coincides with the space occupied by the rest of the physical body. It appears that by following this movement of attention internally, one can see that our physical structure, the head above and the body below, mimics some subjective geometry or anatomy.

I was also struck by the same paradox I encountered with the movement of inside/outside. In that movement, there are two different kinds of reality where attention can direct itself—either the subjective nature of inside or the objective nature of outside. The inside of experience appears to lack substance and the outside appears as objects, substantial and concrete.

With the vertical movement up into thought and down into body, a similar crossing of textural realities takes place. A thought or idea appears as ephemeral and without substance while emotional feeling and sensation appear to be more substantial. In addition, the body can be contacted directly, while the mind majors in symbolic representation. Because of this distinction, the fact of the body is the second skill in our trilogy of practice, and requires deeper exploration before approaching the third skill, releasing oneself from the fiction of the mind.

COMING TO GROUND

I began to use this vertical movement of attention to my advantage as I sat and allowed my attention to drop away from thought and into body sensation until I could feel my feet on the ground. It was similar to consciously taking a deep breath in and then letting it out while feeling the downward sensation this creates. When we let go of how we are holding ourselves, there always seems to be this experience of downward movement or falling until we make contact with the ground that supports what we are letting go to.

It is challenging to let go of thought and try to remain in sensation for any length of time. It takes practice because attention, by habit, wants to continue its movement back into thought whenever it has been assigned somewhere else. We mostly live in this movement—thought to the world and back again into thought—never focusing long enough to feel the body as our ground of being. We have been conditioned to believe that our idea or thought of our self takes precedence over our *felt sense* of self. In this way, we disconnect the two and diminish our awareness of their creative interaction. This is why we begin with developing the skill of grounding ourselves in the fact of the body before challenging the fiction of the mind.

With practice, we can let attention come to rest within the body without surrendering to the pull to move back into thought. Like a glass of water filled with sediment, once left to settle without being shaken, it all settles to the bottom. Without the mind agitating the body's energies, it settles with itself and finds its own ground.

By allowing this settling movement, we can catch the downward movement by relaxing away from thought, and dropping into the sensation of our feet on the floor. It is easy to get caught in the upward movement into the head, but with practice we can get better at letting this happen without resisting it. And when we recognize that we are back in thought, we can shift attention back into body sensation, relax, and follow the downward movement to the feet on the floor.

Once settled and resting in the body, I begin to notice cues that let me know I am entering *embodiment*—a feeling of downward movement, warmth, tingly sensation, and a sense of feeling heavier and more solid. These sensations are always there as feedback, like an experiential pathway that guides us deeper into the experience.

I AM BIGGER THAN I THOUGHT I WAS

An interesting thing begins to happen once we feel settled and are resting in this experience. The internal felt experience of the body begins to expand in size. There is a pervasive quiet and stillness. Instead of attention wanting to move up and down or in and out, it spreads out in many directions until it feels round and larger than the physical body. In sense/felt experience, we begin to join with a field of vibrant awareness. Within this field we can feel the physical body as well as observe the conscious mind and its ever moving content. The mind and the body both seem to belong within the field itself. It is as if, from the field's perspective, the proper alignment is field, to body, to conscious mind and then to our outer perception of the world we see out there. I call this state the *field of energy and awareness beyond the mind/body.*

Being grounded in our point of perception is the doorway or entry point to this state of awareness. It recognizes emerging experience as perceptual in nature, and as the product of the relationship between perceiver and perceived. This field of energy and awareness is a natural location from which to observe the mechanics of our conscious experience before we identify with the outer forms it takes. At the same time, it positions us to sense into the deeper energies of the inner self.

By practicing this simple shift in attention, we are able to experience a shift in consciousness to a state that is more comprehensive. This state *includes* the physical body and the conscious mind, but is *a field of energy and awareness that precedes both.* It is similar to the space I was moved into while the speaking experience was occurring, although not as large or rarified.

While playing more with the movement up and down between being in thought and being in the body, we can notice that the sensation of the body is constant and always there, while the mind is always in movement and changing its content. I call this the *fact of the body.* The body is a subjective fact, but one that can be relied on to be ever present when we turn our attention to it. It is the ground from which we can travel into thought or into the world and yet still return to ourselves because the body never moves out of the present moment.

But the mind is different. When our attention turns to thought, we find that we are either in the past or the future.

Having just left the body poised in the moment, we are now thrust into time. In the mind, we cannot find an equivalent experience for the present, or being in the moment. We can observe the mind producing dialog and pictures about what is happening in the present, but they are still one step removed from the direct perception of right now. It appears as if the mind has no access to the experience of now without joining itself with our sensory experience.

SEPARATE BUT EQUAL

This awareness of how we perceive time and space is important for a number of reasons. First is the separation between mind and body, which we don't fully recognize in normal consciousness. Secondly, mind and body occupy different positions in time. The body is in the now, and the mind, while able to refer to the present, is mostly in the past and the future. These are two locations – mind and body—separate, yet profoundly joined in a cooperative relationship that produces our experience of being in time. Past and future do not exist except as thought.

Only by resting more fully in the field of energy and awareness beyond both the conscious mind and body, can we begin to see their marvelous cooperation in action. You can glimpse this separate yet intrinsically bound relationship between the mind and body by giving yourself the following tasks:

1. Try to experience an emotional hurt without using thought as a way of evoking the feeling. If you find yourself confused as to how to do this, you are doing it right. The precursor to most of our emotional

responses is to recall a circumstance from the past where you felt hurt. Without memory being evoked (memory being a story in narrative and/or pictures held in the mind), the feeling cannot be accessed.

2. Experience excitement without using thought. Again, the mind, as the carrier of past and future, will be put into service. You will once more find yourself reaching for an excitement that occurred in the past or projecting an event that you are anticipating in the future.

3. Make a choice without reference to past and future. Wanting to avoid past mistakes or future perceived consequences dominates our decision process. Without the mind providing its historical catalog of potential outcomes, we fall into doubt and refuse to take the risk of making a choice. We want to be assured of success and avoid the possibility of failure before a choice is made and brought into actualization.

4. Sit with a friend and describe yourself to them without using past and future. This may be difficult to do because our view of who we are is usually built on stories from our past. These mental constructs about who we have been or who we are going to be influence the view of who we are now. Without our stories, we may not know how to think or feel about ourselves.

Our state of being is a result of how these two aspects of our experience, mind and body, cooperate to produce our emotional feelings, our capacity to exercise our will, and even how we construct our view of ourselves.

Resting as the field of energy and awareness beyond the mind and body allows us to separate and explore the different parts of self-experience in order to see how they contribute to the experience of wholeness. It is a misconception that we are bound by time. We are not a being inserted into time; we are a being that produces the perception of time. Time is one of the fictions of the mind. By practicing the first and second skills, we start to uncover the third skill—releasing ourselves from the fiction of the mind.

The separateness of inside/outside, mind/body and past/future is now experienced as a function of perception. The conscious self, while appearing to be constrained by time and space, is actually using time and space to create for its own purposes.

LOCATING OUR POINT OF PERCEPTION

By following the natural movements of our attention, we have been able to locate our point of perception in both space and time. It is located in space as the experience of *in here* as compared to *out there*, along the horizontal line we discovered when playing with inside/outside. Our point of perception in time follows the vertical line that moves up into thought (past and future) and down into the body, and is always present as the experience of now.

This intersection between space and time is our point of perception, the center point and middle ground between our outer perceived reality and the deeper energies of our larger consciousness. It has been hidden just outside our awareness, resting all along in the *here and now*. We are able to access thoughts, feelings, and sensations along with the more subtle energy dimensions of a deeper self from this location.

The movements of attention along the horizontal and vertical axis are going on all the time. Granting them our attention and following them moves us to a natural center deeper in the Self from which we can observe and experience our ever-expanding inner landscape. This point of perception is now available and ready to offer up its mysteries.

CHAPTER 14

INHABITING YOUR ESSENCE

In western thought, the concept of *essence* is defined as the attribute, or set of attributes, that make an entity or substance what it fundamentally is, and without which it loses its identity. I am using the word essence to point to an attribute that is basic and invariable within our self-experience—our self-awareness.

In the preface to this book, I made the statement that while we all have the *capacity* for self-awareness, to actually *be in* a state of self-awareness is a different order of experience. I am using the expression *inhabiting your essence,* to indicate the latter – an experience where we are occupying and living in a state of self-awareness and where this essential attribute is being fully used and realized in the service of our greatest potential.

I am making the distinction state of self-awareness to highlight what begins to happen when we locate our point of perception in the here and now, settle into the body and enter the field of energy and awareness that exists beyond the body. In our ordinary state of consciousness the content of our thoughts, feelings and sensations are identified as belonging to the perceiver. When we inhabit this state of self-awareness, the identification with content is released and one experiences the self separate and free from it. We can then recognize that it is awareness itself that is the primary ground of being. This is the experience of *being in* a state of self-awareness as compared to *having* self-awareness. From this state, the mind and body and their relationship to a larger whole become observable in a new and creative way that allows new experience to emerge.

PLAYING WITH MY INNER LANDSCAPE

While engaged in my daily life, I continued to make clearer distinctions within my experience as I shifted my attention along the vertical line, the up and down movement between thought and the body. I let my attention go deeper into the body and the field of energy within which it rests. Keeping my focus on sensation, I had a more subtle experience of *energetic awareness*, i.e., the experience of naturally connecting to a larger field of awareness when we are centered and grounded in our point of perception.

We can bring this practice into the actions of daily life, at any time and in any circumstance. Like the monk using his mantra or prayer beads, we can practice being awake and responsible for where our attention is focused and the ground it occupies in direct experience, in the here and now.

FINDING A PLACE TO PRACTICE

Any student learning these skills can find areas in their lives where they can practice, whether it's during the mundane activities they encounter throughout their day or special areas of interest they are pursuing. Physical activities are great opportunities for practice. Washing dishes, vacuuming, mowing the lawn, lifting, reaching and running all provide the opportunity to be aware of the vertical axis, falling from thought into body, settling into sensation and allowing the appropriate energies to fit the activity. Other places to practice are those leisure activities where you have already developed some mastery, or are able to perform with little self-consciousness so that you can play with shifting your focus while doing them. In this way your daily life activities become the medium you use to experience your point of perception and the experience of inhabiting your own center; from there you can observe what it is like to be a participant in generating your state of being.

There were three main activities in my life that I began to use to give myself special practice time each week; sitting with Ellen in meditation; working with clay in my studio; and working with clients in my counseling practice. Each of these activities demands a state of presence in order to meet the task at hand; each also draws upon qualities of my consciousness that are central to my evolving nature. I will share them with you in the following chapters to show how to practice, and what can happen when we bring together our life activities with the practice of shifting states.

PRACTICING IN RELATIONSHIP

Over the years, Ellen and I have continued sitting together as we did in Hawaii, exploring the subtle realms of higher energy states and their practical as well as profound impact on our ordinary consciousness. Occupying the center of our life is our relationship with one another. We enjoy the experience of creative outflow and the shared intimacy of being in expanded states together. This creates a bond between us that transcends our separateness and deepens our love for one another. Our meeting in higher states is instrumental in supporting us to process the ups and downs of relationship.

During our day, Ellen and I often drop what we are doing and go and sit in two chairs facing each other. We settle down the vertical axis, let go of thought and become present within sensation. Like the sediment in a glass of water surrendering to the pull of gravity, our attention comes to rest at our seat in the chair, our back against the back of the chair and our feet on the ground, as if responding to an equivalent, yet subjective, force of gravity.

After a few minutes of resting in these three points of sensation, they converge and unite to produce the experience of feeling the body as one unit, the parts joining to produce the whole. Once the experience of the body as a whole is accepted into awareness, the process repeats itself by starting to produce glimpses of the next state. We may feel tingling and heat, or a softening of the boundaries of the physical body as the energy field begins to move into awareness. If these first intrusions of the next state into our awareness are not accepted and acknowledged, awareness continues to circulate within its current state. There appears to be an inherent desire within the multidimensional levels of the self to move toward larger comprehension and experience. We then move into the experience of the field. Within this experience, and depending on our intention, we can explore its properties and relationship to even larger states and observe the relationships between the energy field, the conscious mind, the body and the world.

Our intentions also vary. Often we sit with no intention except to receive instruction and wisdom from the state. This leads to frequent explorations into expanded states where information, knowledge or direct experience is received.

Within these layers of consciousness we meet new qualities of being and perception and absorb their point of view and unique form of organization.

THE COMMITTED VISITOR

I always leave these experiences feeling like a *committed visitor*. I am committed by the obvious fact that I am alive in a physical body and subject to all the laws pertaining to physical reality. At the same time, my subjective experience is multidimensional, giving me direct experience that transcends the body and the conscious self with which I identify. This subjective part of me does not belong to physical reality. It enjoys my body and its physical realties as a visitor might. I am free to come and go. As I investigate further, I come to appreciate deeply that we are all committed visitors and that this is our natural state of being.

At other times Ellen and I receive reincarnation material where I find myself at the center of a circle, with strands of light moving towards particular positions on its outer rim. If I follow one out, I am aware of a protagonist in another time and place. I can choose to be the witness, or enter into the action as the main character and experience from its point of view.

This type of experience always leads back to me in the present and shows the genesis of personal qualities, preferences and points of view that are either supportive or limiting to my current self. From these experiences, I have gained a deeper appreciation for the dream I had about being an artist. The transfer or sharing of qualities across time and through dimensions only hints at the creativity that is always going on beneath our everyday consciousness.

I believe that all these energy forms are open and accessible to being known and engaged with. Our exchanges are always enlightening and rewarding. It is inspiring to realize that the inside of experience is as populated with life, circumstance and meaning as our outer experience. Unfortunately, this view is profoundly absent from contemporary Western culture. Our scientific point of view, while creating technological wonders on the outside, has left the inside unknowable to us, dead and barren as a source of meaning and vision.

PRACTICE IS PRACTICAL

Ellen and I also sit together to solve problems. If we need clarity about a decision we have to make, or directions we need to take, we sit together, shift to a more expanded state and open to new views on the matter from a more comprehensive state. We also experiment with unlocking the emotional conflicts that take place between us. When we find ourselves arguing or in disagreement, we stop the action, go sit in our chairs across from one another and shift into a more settled state, one in which we can feel our own contraction and upset. Each of us accepts the energy of our own reactive state instead of acting it out on the other. Doing this shifts the dynamic between us and allows us to negotiate a satisfying resolution.

These are some of the many ways and circumstances we use to integrate this new level of consciousness, and attempt to transform the activities of daily life into a new perception—one that is more playful, open, and creative. New patterns of understanding are discovered and become available for addressing the practical issues we meet in our life.

These higher states are *always* present but remain undetected and outside of normal awareness. But when the quality of our normal consciousness is altered, these new forms of knowledge and experience become accessible and allow us to generate new distinctions. Distinctions make things visible that were invisible before. Differentiation creates new possibilities of being. A body of distinctions constitutes a deepening of experience. As new thought is generated out of new experience, that thought is reintroduced and produces even more new observations and new distinctions.

This is a common experience for anyone who masters a skill, craft or art. When you begin learning a new skill, the complexities seem overwhelming. But as you continue to practice, these same complexities begin to make sense and offer new possibilities not seen before. This is true whether you are learning to drive a car, play baseball, use a computer or play guitar. It is true whether the activity is physical, emotional or intellectual. You enter its world and if you practice, that world will open and makes itself known to you through the body of distinctions that exist within it.

The same dynamic is true when practicing self-awareness. It just so happens that the instrument we are learning to play is the known and familiar self. With practice, the field of experience becomes more layered and subtle. There is a *dynamic reciprocity* that seems to characterize the relationship between all levels of the self, a giving and receiving that joins each to the other.

As I went back and read some of the notes from my speaking experience in Hawaii, I ran across the following statement,

"What you are doing is learning and practicing an art, the art of being with yourself and your experience in a way that keeps opening to multidimensional experience. An art requires practice to become natural. Practice reorganizes the self that is practicing. The experience that the practice elicits in you changes the self and thus evolves you.

You are being invited to play with your ability to shift your attention from one area of your experience to another. It is important to know that you have the ability to choose to pay attention within the self. Often experience happens so quickly that one simply goes along for the ride. An aspect of this practice will be to exercise your ability to choose to attend, and how to attend, to facilitate an expanded state.

It is in the realm of sensing that the internal landscape of the Self will become available to you as a resource. This resource allows you to know your own nature, and to utilize the Self more effectively in daily life. In order to bring these capacities forward into consciousness, you have to cultivate them."

CHAPTER 15

SPINNING TO EXPAND

PLAYING WITH FORCE FIELDS

When I am in my clay studio, which is in the garage or some other outbuilding separate from our living area, I am always excited about setting up my physical space. To support the process of creating a piece from start to finish, I use setting up as preparation to engage with the clay so that I can bring something into being that didn't exist before.

Working with clay is exciting for me for a number of reasons. The first is physical. Working with clay, particularly on the potter's wheel, is an exercise in grounding myself in the body in order to perform the functions required. The second reason is that the entire process of working with clay is a metaphor for how I am engaged within my consciousness and what I am attempting to bring into my daily life.

Throwing on the wheel is a graphic out-picturing of how to organize myself from energy field, to body, to world and back again—the constant interplay between parts of the self that cooperate together to manifest an event or experience. So it is with turning a lump of earth into a beautiful, functional or decorative piece of fine art. I learn how I treat myself by how I treat the clay. It is a process of becoming more self-aware; it is my most concrete form of practice. Any physical skill that you do repetitively can serve this purpose.

I first wedge the clay in order to remove all air pockets and hard knots that might exist. Wedging, which is like kneading dough, requires a rhythmic rocking back and forth movement best done from the feet and hips. Otherwise you end up using your shoulders and make the task harder by separating yourself from the source of the power needed to do the job. Just like Tai Chi, Qigong or other martial arts, I have to organize my body in relationship to the energy field that precedes it so the energy flow can be used and directed with ease.

Throwing is all about touch and flow and so is making contact with the world. Presence is a felt sense in the body, not the mind. When we lean too heavily on our interpretations or concepts about the world, we end up wedging the world from our shoulders, making it harder and removing ourselves from the source of direct contact. Our conscious mind can only touch its own symbols for the world, whereas the body and its energy field touches more directly the energy before the world takes form.

Once the clay is ready, I sit down and place it in the center of the wheel and turn on the wheel. This is always the moment of truth. I am aware of an object spinning within its own force field and I have to prepare myself to enter this centrifugal force field in such a way that I can use its movement to create in accordance with my will and intention. Again, the metaphor of stepping into a world of my creation is never lost on me. I am excited and anxious simultaneously.

Earlier I used the term—*committed visitor*—to describe our unique dual nature. We are beings who find ourselves committed by birth to physical existence and the laws that govern its mechanics. This is our objective stance in the world and its laws dictate how the surface of things move and relate. At the same time, we are visitors who are not bound subjectively to these mechanics. We transcend them daily by traveling within our subjective universe, exiting time and space in sleep, dreams, imagination and all the subtle shifts of consciousness that place us outside its influence.

I revisit the concept here because facing the force of the spinning wheel is a wonderful metaphor for the way we navigate through life. I cannot escape having to deal with the force of the wheel if I want to use its movement to create form. I have to commit, just as I must commit to my life as a physical being in a physical world. Now, the question is; what do I do with the force operating on me and within me?

CENTER TO CENTER

I have to reach into this force field, make contact with the clay and move it into the direct center of the spinning wheel. When this happens, the clay finds its center within the field and spins calmly and balanced under my hands. This is a perfect mimic of what it feels like when I drop away from thought into the body, and into the field of energy and awareness that precedes it.

In order to move the clay into its center, I first have to find my own center. I have to connect my center to the center of the wheel so that I can feel where the spinning clay is in relationship to its center. This is my practice. When I shift from thought, to feeling, to energy flow, the path to this shared center becomes visible. Once the clay is centered, I can begin to create with it, using the spinning of the wheel to pull a form into being.

Meanwhile, I also have to keep withdrawing my hands from the clay, wet them, and then re-enter its force field, in order to keep it moist with water so that it can spin under my hands with ease. These in and out movements must be done with sensitivity or the clay will be knocked off center, and any attempt to create from off center has consequences. This happens often, so a lot of time is spent finding my own center again and then using this felt sense to re-center the clay. I am constantly involved in correcting my mistakes. If I become too aggressive in trying to compensate for my mistakes, I throw the clay more off center. What a metaphor for life! Instead of getting tight to correct, I have to let go, center again, and feel my way back into contact with the clay. I can then regain control and continue to create.

I often sit at the wheel shaking my head, on the verge of laughter or hysteria, with clay and water dripping off me as a consequence of attempting to impose my will on the clay. The more I push, the more off center everything becomes. The clay, the wheel and their force field all demand that I be in harmony with them or I cannot create within the universe they occupy. I have to learn this lesson over and over again until I begin to understand that I have no control over the forces operating on me until I come to terms with the forces operating within me and through me.

CHAPTER 16

LISTENING INTO UNION

BEFORE THE SPLIT INTO ME AND INTO YOU

I n my work with clients, I constantly drew on the new distinctions in awareness I was discovering and practicing. Meeting someone at the point of his or her suffering always brings me into the here and now and deepens my state of receptivity. My sittings with Ellen were excursions into spirit; my work with clay was my physical energetic practice; my work with clients was my opportunity to explore the heart of compassion that lies under the confusion and turbulence we experience at the surface of ourselves.

I began to practice listening from the field of energy and awareness that precedes the mind and body, the interface between deeper realities of self and conscious experience. It is a state of consciousness where reality takes on more flexibility, openness and permeability. As stated earlier, this state of consciousness is a location within subjectivity; it is characterized by its access to both the outside and inside of experience and to a more comprehensive self-awareness.

Listening from a different location within myself was hard at first. I had to learn to do something I thought I already knew how to do. Like walking, speaking and seeing, listening seemed effortless and automatic. It is so natural that it is often unconsciously performed. When we do give the act of listening our attention, it is usually because we want to correct or solve a problem that is showing up between ourselves and others. How we hear what they have to say is often self-protective and predicated on self-interest.

To learn how to really *hear* the *person* who is speaking to us, instead of just hearing the words they are saying, is a different order of listening and connection. As I practiced shifting my state, I became aware of doing many more things then just hearing the person speak. I discovered that I had made myself separate from the person; therefore they couldn't truly be heard. My intention was to close the gap between speaker and listener so that meaning became a shared experience where we could move into communion. I became aware that, embedded in the way I listened, there were assumptions or positions that closed down the possibility of the connection I was after.

WHO AM I HEARING?

I discovered that I was treating the person speaking as if they were me, expecting to hear *my* experience reflected in their speaking. My ear was already attuned to hearing what was familiar and meaningful to me. Just like my eyes skipped over novel objects to land on familiar sights, so my hearing was likewise conditioned to favor what was already known in meaning. I didn't listen for what the person's speaking meant to *them*, I listened for what it meant to *me*. When the speaker said what *they* meant, I was expecting it to mean what it meant to *me*.

From this positioning, a number of further assumptions followed naturally. For example, I assumed my reaction to their communication resided in their speaking instead of in my listening. I displaced the burden of my reaction onto them. I believed that my reactions to the speaker accurately reflected the speaker's statements. In fact they didn't; they more accurately reflected my interpretation of the speaker's statements.

One of the most common ways most of us separate from whom we are listening to is to think the speaker is describing an objective world instead of a subjective one. This leads to questioning the authenticity of what the speaker is saying because we hold our own experience to be the standard by which we assess the *truth* of their statements. For example, when my partner says, "Boy, it sure is hot in here" and I respond with, "I don't think so, I'm not hot," it is as if her speaking requested a comparison with my own experience instead of being a statement of hers.

Because we share a common language, we expect our words to point to a commonly shared objective reality. They don't. What we are attempting to do when we speak is use common meaning to describe our idiosyncratic experience. We can only use language to approximate what we mean; the rest is in the listening.

To put it another way, I discovered that what I was hearing was not the speaker, but myself. I was caught in what I call reactive listening. My attention and awareness was centered on my response and reaction to what was being said. While this awareness is critical to good communication and allows one to own their half of the dance, it is only a part of the action possible. I needed to get over myself and reach the person who was speaking. Being entranced by my own responses was separating me from hearing the experience of the person speaking. Their intention in speaking was to be heard and received, understood and accepted, just as they are, the way they experience themselves. This is something we all hope for, and motivates us to communicate in the first place.

As I practiced shifting my center of attention from mind to body, and then into the field of energy that precedes them, I began to have a new experience of what it was like to really hear the person sitting across from me. This state of consciousness demonstrated a conceptual flexibility and an energetic openness I didn't possess in my ordinary consciousness.

In our normal everyday state, the conscious mind creates a concept from raw and discrete sense data. This data is offered up to the mind as color, texture, smell, taste, temperature, sound, dimension, and function. The mind finds the appropriate category or concept to fit this discrete data and organizes it so it can be named or labeled and thus become a thing. We then begin to perceive the 'object' instead of registering the sensory information of which it is composed. This conceptual object then begins to dominate our experience. We end up living in a world of objects instead of the raw sensory experiences that make it up.

This was the inner message I heard while standing on the deck in Hawaii, inviting me to go inside to a world that was not yet named. The inside was still open to be experienced directly, prior to the conscious mind's turning it into concepts and objects.

In contrast to reactive listening, this state of energy and awareness doesn't come to conclusions or make judgments. It stays in process, conceptually open and flexible to the stream of meaning that the speaker conveys through gesture, tone and language. Instead of taking what is said and building a concept around it, it observes and apprehends how the speaker is constructing their perceived reality in the moment. But if listening is filtered through my mind, I can only hear what I want to hear, expect to hear or am conditioned to hear.

Another attribute of conscious listening is energetic openness. I began to experience this while listening to clients. I didn't have to leave my center to join with them. It was as if my center expanded to include theirs, connecting with the energetic state of the speaker as they spoke themselves into being. Like the clay on the wheel, I must join center to center. It was palpable and energetic, as if we shared the same space, immediate and direct. I felt the emotional energy evoked by their creation and followed what they did with it, i.e., either accepting it, or moving to protect themselves from its intrusion.

I have had many experiences where the boundary between myself and another disappears, leaving me to register directly the inside of their experience as they experienced it themselves. A wonderful shared experience of profound intimacy and hysterical laugher often followed these moments, always ending with the client's deep appreciation for being seen, just as they are.

After one intense experience, I remembered something from my notes of the original speaking experience and found this statement:

"The nature of awareness itself is to attune to what is held in its presence. You are practicing a natural capacity for relationship that exists throughout consciousness and is the cooperative foundation upon which it rests."

CHAPTER 17

THE RETURN OF
THE SPEAKER

IT'S ONLY ME

Whether I was sitting, throwing clay or working with clients, my days were filled with discovery and energy. My ability to shift rapidly and smoothly between states increased until it was only a thought away. Having each state of thought, body and energy field distinguished clearly in experience made the movement between them easy and effortless. When I rested in the field, my body and conscious mind still remained present in the experience. This was not true when all of my attention was focused in thought; in that instance, I no longer had awareness of the body and the field. In contrast, the larger awareness represented by the energy field always included the heavier vibrational fields of mind and body. If my attention

125

identified with one of these heavier fields, I lost awareness of the larger experience.

When I began as a seeker reading the accounts of others who sought higher states of consciousness, I assumed that when they gained entrance into a higher state they were transformed, awakened and subsequently lived in that state all the time. That was my misconception.

In order to remain in a particular state, attention has to be present within it. The dynamic nature of the multi-dimensional self and the life force energy it uses and processes constantly moves attention around unless one takes conscious control of its movement. This is why my first skill was to learn to move with it or take control of its direction. The goal is not to hold a state against the forces operating upon it, but to be able to move freely within it and through it.

My access to higher states did not move me above life but allowed me to be facile within it. The subjective geography I have described made this possible. I knew where to go with my attention to be present to thought, to feel an emotional feeling, to organize sensation in the body, or to evoke an elevated state. When confronted with the issues in my life, I was able to work more skillfully with myself and come to resolutions that were harmless to myself and others.

The more perceptually integrated I became, the more I became myself. It was as if I had only been aware of a small part of my self, yet in the background was a field of being that held all of the particular energies related to me and now moved them forward into conscious awareness.

I began to see that a perceptual integration not only described the coming together of parts within a state, but also the joining or union between states, one with the other.

SHARING THE PRACTICE

Over time I wondered if the body of distinctions I was practicing could be taught and applied to others. As my self-awareness expanded, I began to introduce my clients to parts of the process that seemed relevant in the moment. This always resulted in positive movement and a clarity that allowed the person to release energy that was being used to hold him or her in place. The more I did this, the more I began to see the need for this type of learning.

The absence of self-awareness is not a therapeutic issue. It is an educational one. Each of us has the capacity for self-awareness built into our nature but inclination and circumstance have limited its exercise. As children we are never given the tools necessary to be skillful *within* ourselves. All of our socialization is directed at the interface between our behavior and the world, leaving our subjective self to flounder in doubt and mistrust over its own validity.

I decided to experiment by bringing together a group of interested people to share the shifts in consciousness I was practicing. I began by teaching the three basic skills I had been using to guide my own learning; taking control of attention, grounding in the fact of the body and releasing from the fiction of the mind. As this first training and subsequent classes demonstrated, these are not only teachable skills but skills that are universal in impact on those who practice them. The outer results are always idiosyncratic.

What is universal is the increase and expansion of consciousness and self-awareness that results from being engaged in the act of turning attention inward and using it to explore the nature of self-experience.

My impulse to experiment with teaching these skills had two results I had not anticipated, yet which represented the fulfillment of the original experience begun in Hawaii. The first was upon my outer life. After the success of the first training, I taught another and then another until over the next twenty-five years, teaching became an integral and important part of my life. From private groups to public workshops, institutional and corporate trainings to university classes, I have had the opportunity to explore with thousands of people the excitement and wonder of self-exploration through self-awareness.

Teaching was the fulfillment of the vision that had been implicit in the speaking experience when it stated:

"It is now time to bring forward into conscious awareness the knowledge and direct perception of self that these inner senses provide. These areas of your being, while existing in silence, wait patiently for you to give them life as they give you life moment to moment. Perception grants beingness. Within each individual, inherent in their nature, exist the organs of perception that, when used and activated, will give birth to a new and more expanded self-experience."

COMING AWAKE

The second consequence of deciding to teach was its effect on my inner life. One morning, after teaching my first class, I woke from sleep into an unusual experience. I felt as if I was being held in the space between sleep and wake-fulness by some unseen force. I drifted between these two states, unable to reach the surface of wakefulness as I kept being pulled back into a dreamy awareness. For moments I was in a dream, then I was pushed out into a more conscious awake state, though I was not fully awake. I was aware of the movement back and forth; it seemed as if I was being shown the territory I was travelling between for a reason.

Later I began to receive a series of concepts and prac-tices that pertained to the teaching material I was using in the class I was teaching at the time. Sensed images, with their meaning fully realized, would reach my conscious awareness while in this state of waking up. If I drifted too close to being fully awake, I began to lose their meaning as the conscious mind tried to translate them into what it already knew. When this happened, I allowed myself to fall back into the deeper state from which they came and they reappeared. After some time passed, I felt myself, like a rescue buoy, popping up from the depths and breaking the surface, fully awake.

This experience taught me that the process of waking up is important. We enter back into our conscious form af-ter a nightly journey outside of time and space. As we wake up, the thoughts, feelings and views experienced outside of form are being translated into form and leave a conscious residue. The conditioned mind quickly co-opts this mate-rial and turns it into recognizable information congruent with the waking self's view.

We all experience this state each morning before our conscious mind takes control of our process and we begin to turn our attention to the projected events of the coming day. It is what sleep researchers call the *hypnopompic state*, a powerful period when our awareness moves back into engaging with the outer senses and we take on form again. Because we are coming into form instead of letting go of it, we are very receptive to inspirational material and promptings from the deeper self.

It had been a number of years since the speaking experience had come to an end, yet this experience had the same feel and same focus of content, the delivery of wisdom and knowledge across dimensional boundaries, one state of consciousness to another. And like the speaking experience, it continued. Each morning this state offered itself to me as a place to support what I was engaged in, broadening its scope far beyond teaching to include other areas of my life.

Unlike the speaking experience however, my waking up experiences have not ended; they continue to this day. Along the way I have learned to use them consciously by choosing to linger between sleep and wakefulness each morning, bringing the promise of new knowledge and understanding before I meet the world once again.

I have come full circle, beginning with the speaking experience in Hawaii, which moved me from an experience of separateness into a more expanded relationship with my self, a natural cooperative relationship that continues to unfold and reveal my essence. When we left Hawaii, I had few doubts about how difficult it was going to be to maintain the state of consciousness I was enjoying, let alone how to continue to deepen it in the face of a daily life much different than the retreat environment that had aided its emergence. The speaking had addressed this and then disappeared as an outer phenomenon and support.

Thankfully, it has now returned and lives as an internal aspect of my experience, one I continue to cultivate, access and use in my everyday life.

PART THREE

MANAGING YOUR STATE OF BEING

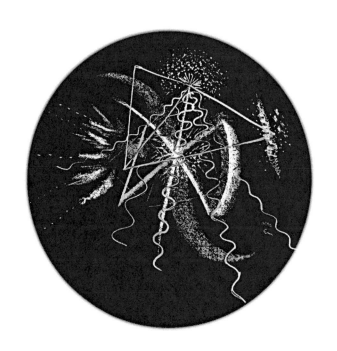

CHAPTER 18

THE MIND AS WE KNOW IT

While the practice of taking control of attention and grounding in the fact of the body led me into the adventures in consciousness described in the previous chapters, it is the third skill in my trilogy of practice—*releasing oneself from the fiction of the mind* – that consolidated and stabilized my experience in everyday life.

The more time I spent in the energy fields that precede our normal experience of mind and body, the more I began to experience my self and its operations from a different point of view. From this elevated perspective, I experienced the self as a creative and dynamic system of energy in motion, which replaced my psychological view of self as an object with a constellation of attributes that form a personality profile. Instead of being contained and confined within a closed system of attributes and characteristics that are carried through time, I experienced myself as

135

an *open* system, multidimensional, constantly in motion and profoundly creative in generating itself in the moment.

Previously, I had established a working model of my experience that I called my personal geography, while I explored controlling my attention and grounding myself in the fact of the body. This model was helpful as I practiced these skills. It left a trail of concepts and directions that I could follow and revise as my experience continued, keeping me current and in alignment with the action as it unfolded. I now proceeded to do the same with the skill of releasing myself from the fiction of the mind. I started building a new working model out of my experience with the energy field that precedes the mind and body. This offered me a larger and more comprehensive view of the mind and the cooperative role it plays in constructing our state of being. The following assumptions became my working model:

- Everything is consciousness.
- Consciousness appears as energy in all of its possible forms.
- As a human being, we are one of the forms this energy takes.
- This human energy appears to us in the form of body, mind and spirit.
- Body, mind and spirit work together as a dynamic energy system to produce a living picture and experience of self that constitutes our state of being. It is the sum of our experience in any moment.
- The dynamic relationship between body, mind and spirit is set into constant motion by our *perceptual*

interpretation of what is seen as real for us in the moment.

- As body, mind and spirit, we are an open and intelligent energy system that works to produce and generate awareness of itself.

- Using this capacity to know ourselves through self-awareness, we can learn and evolve ourselves as a creative act of consciousness.

WE ARE OLD AND NEW SIMULTANEOUSLY

Viewed from our everyday experience, the conscious mind is both the repository of old ideas carried through time, and the space in which new ideas appear. We are both conditioned and intuitive. We are programmed by habits of thought and, at the same time, are able to be transformed by new vision, inspiration and revelation. This is just one of the many paradoxes that characterize our nature.

Between the world of outer perception and the inner world of intuitive knowing lies the conscious mind, as we experience it. It contains all the ideas and beliefs that have been generated by our contact and interaction with the life we lead. Our beliefs represent the clustering of ideas around the conclusions we have reached about the nature of our particular reality. We use them as functional guidelines to maneuver through our lives. Our conditioning is the habit of entering an experience already organized to interpret it in a way that confirms our current view. Said simply, we see what we expect to see.

These beliefs are also used by the inner self as a lens through which we project an out-picturing of our private world onto the screen of our public sight. In this way, we know ourselves from the inside and meet ourselves on the outside through an act of perception. This is a truly marvelous construction.

While the intuitive mind expands our world, the conditioned mind contracts us and holds us in place. When I was learning how to manage my own state of being, it was the conditioned part of the mind that I wanted to release myself from. I didn't try to change, correct or alter it in any way. I was more interested in releasing myself from being at the effect of the conditioned mind. To achieve this, I held the mind in awareness while sitting in meditation in the field of energy and awareness that precedes the mind and body, an elevated state that provided enough separation from the mind's activity so that I could observe and be less identified with it.

OUR STORY

In my daily life I also practiced being grounded in the body, which enabled me to observe the mind's activity more clearly and be less confused about whether I was in thought or not. Playing with the vertical axis of attention and knowing the difference between being in my head versus my body was an important part of this process.

Life comes to us as a result of our direct sensory experience in the moment. At the same time, and appearing to share the same space, there is a continuous stream of mental interpretation and comment offered by the mind. I call the latter *our story* about our experience. The mind creates a story about our experience, using the pool of sensory information at its disposal. It is what the conscious mind is built for, to produce and offer symbolic meaning to the moment of experience. The mind presents our story in two primary ways: the first is internal narrative—the constant verbal conversation that goes on within our minds. The second is an internal out-picturing, the flow of images and pictures projected before the mind's eye.

We live in this world of inner narrative and out-picturing as much as we live in the physical world of our senses. In fact, we have a difficult time telling these two parts of self-experience apart because they seem to arrive simultaneously and fit so seamlessly together. We don't recognize that they come from two distinct parts of the self – the mind and the body. When they are collapsed into each other, the possibility of identifying ourselves as our mind and our body is increased, and self-awareness is diminished. We become bound and subject to our own definition of who we are.

For example, when our story is left unconscious and unexamined, it can create some of the following dilemmas that propel us deeper into a conditioned and often contracted state:

- We believe our story is true (fact) instead of being a creation (fiction) on our part. We mistake fiction for fact.
- When we deny authorship of our story and hold it as fact, we deny responsibility. We diminish the possibility for accurate feedback regarding our own creation.

- When our story lives as a fact, we become subject to it, we are at the effect of it. It is unseen and we assign it to the objective world. It is now a belief about our selves or the world. Our story is now living us.

- When our story is supported by belief, it is held as true and right, and ultimately becomes the standard by which we move ourselves into judgment and separation.

- We become attached to the drama inherent in our own story, and are now engaged in its maintenance for a sense of vitality and authenticity.

- We carry our story through time, allowing the content that was generated from the past to dominate the present and predict the future. This results in becoming subject to linear time instead of using past and future as tools of creation in an expanding present.

AT THE EFFECT OF MYSELF

As time passed, I became more aware of the internal narratives and out-picturing process that dominated my everyday consciousness. I knew this was important in helping me discover where I was most subject to my conditioning and at the effect of my story about my experience. I gave full attention to the inner narratives and pictures instead of engaging with them in a half conscious way or moving away from them out of apprehension or distrust. I wanted to have a relationship with these aspects of my experience and bring them into conscious awareness.

It was important for me to become aware of the view of reality that my internal dialogue and pictures produced, since they were translated into perceptions that created my view of my self and the world. They helped organize me into the reality I knew. As I began to recognize the presence of story, I saw it everywhere in my experience.

For example, after interacting with someone, I would tell myself stories about who they were and why they acted as they did. When circumstances flowed to my advantage or didn't, I would have a story as to why it had or hadn't, or why it could have been different. When I contemplated taking an action, I had a story for why it would be successful or not and predicated my actions on its narrative. I had stories for my likes and dislikes, my aversions and attractions, my successes and failures and my desires, wants and intentions. I existed in a sea of continuous assessment and judgment that explained or justified my actions whether in behavior, thought or feeling, and provided the field of meaning out of which I acted and made sense of what I encountered.

As I developed a greater interest in observing the *process* of my story and less interest in its content, I discovered numerous underlying patterns that at first had not been visible. For example, the use of linear time appeared to be implicit to my conditioned story telling. My memory of the past was used to explain and justify the present. For instance, I'd experience a feeling of loneliness and then hear a whole narrative about how I moved from place to place as a kid and that's why I was lonely. I didn't initially see that the narrative had moved me from having an authentic feeling in the moment to suffering a state or circumstance from the past that was no longer true in the present. However, because the feeling and the thought occurred simultaneously, this only confirmed my belief that the story was true.

In order to make this dynamic visible, I created some questions to clarify and make the story more accessible. I would write down a recurring negative feeling I experienced. Then I would write down the story I told myself about why I had this feeling. I found that I always had such a story.

I would write down a judgment I had of myself. Then I would write down the story I told myself about why I was this way. I always had a story that explained and justified the assessment or judgment I had of myself. I noticed that the future was also used in my storytelling to control and contain the present and to keep me safe, even though *safe* means *the same,* depleting me of novelty and the vitality it produces. I would watch as I used prediction, anticipation and perceived consequences as the main ways in which I used the future to shape the present.

For example, I would be on my way to a business meeting with associates and find myself predicting how each person would respond to the proposals under discussion. Anticipating their responses, I was preparing myself to react to these predicted responses, thus reducing any tension I was feeling about having to face uncertainty. Or, Ellen might show me a website or brochure of a place we are thinking of taking a vacation. I would immediately begin to hear narratives about what it would be like if we went there, and that would generate feelings of disinterest or excitement, depending on the narrative I was listening to. I would anticipate the experience and predicate my decision about wanting to go on this information.

This pattern was habitual with my mate, with friends and even with me. I would hear narratives predicting how they or I would be in a future circumstance I was envisioning at the moment. My story always supported my feelings of apprehension and anxiety or joy and excitement.

I watched myself making decisions. If there was a decision I wanted to make, but was refraining from, I observed the pictures and narratives I projected about possible outcome flash through my mind. My story about the perceived consequences of making the decision, along with the associated feelings that followed, was fiction masquerading as fact. Once they were perceived as fact, I had no room in which to make the decision. Why make a decision I knew was going to be unsuccessful or painful?

The following is another example of this dynamic, one that was a precursor for me in becoming suspicious that the voice in my head was not telling me the truth of my experience. For many years I was a student of Aikido, a martial art that focuses on using your attacker's energy to defeat them.

One morning, I had just woken up and was thinking about getting ready to go to a morning class. I felt warm and cozy in my bed when I heard a voice in my head say, "What are you doing? You're not going to get up and go to class. If you go to class, you will be thrown around, have your extremities grabbed and twisted and be thrown to the mat over and over again. That will not feel good. Why not just stay where you are and skip class today?" Now, the voice had enough truth on its side to capture my attention. Those things it said would happen in class do actually happen. The voice did represent my past experience, but it was predicting how I would feel and respond in class in a future that had not yet happened.

I don't know how I arrived at the decision to get up and go to class, but I did. Once in class I began to train with my fellow students. I was throwing and being thrown to the mat over and over again. I loved it, every minute of it. The more present I became in my body, the more the falling and pounding and twisting felt wonderful.

At one point during the class, I remembered that I had almost decided to skip class because of the warning voice in my head. In that moment, I had a mini revelation. The voice was not accurate in its prediction of how I would feel in class. It was just a story. The mind can't speak the truth of my future experience because it can only use what it has to work with—symbols and images that represent past experience. As a result, I saw that the mind could not be trusted to give me accurate information about what I will experience in the present or the future. It was an important realization as I continued to explore the role that story plays in my experience.

I began to realize that my indecisiveness could now be seen, not as a personality flaw, but more as an improper use of the future. I saw that the future was a mental construct that could be used to contain and contract me, or extend and expand me. When this was recognized in awareness, the future became a creative tool at my disposal. I could use it to consciously support me in shaping and organizing the present moment and release myself from the fiction of the mind.

Once I accepted that the mind was giving me fiction in the form of fact, my resistance to its input dissolved. Instead of a relationship build on facts being presented to me that I had to accept or resist, agree or disagree, surrender to or deny, my conscious mind became a friend, that part of my self that offered possibilities, some worth considering and others not, about the reality I was facing. I could now use it to support my will and my intentions in living. If we take ourselves to be who we think we are instead of the new emergent self in the moment of direct experience, we continue to carry our story through time, allowing the content generated from the past to dominate the present and predict the future. We become subject to linear time instead of living in an expanding present that uses past and future as tools for creating. When we understand that it is the self in the present moment that uses past and future for its own creative purposes, we see how we can use time to either support our current desires or undermine the possibilities for their realization.

CHAPTER 19

FILLING IN THE WORLD

LEAVING NO SPACE

A friend's experience illustrates a second pattern of storytelling in action. My friend was interested in finding a romantic partner, so she joined an Internet dating service. This resulted in a lunch date with a man also seeking to connect with someone. The lunch went quite well, and they decided to meet again. She liked him a lot and gave him her number. He said he would call her in a few days to make arrangements for another date.

As the days passed without hearing from him, she grew anxious and upset. After a week passed with no call from him, she became depressed and despondent. When I asked what it meant to her that he hadn't called, she immediately launched into a story about how he had lied to her about his interest in seeing her again, and that men were dishonest and untrustworthy.

She finished by saying that it was probably better this way as she was not prepared for relationship and besides, no one would be interested in her anyway. The day after we talked he called. After apologizing for not being in contact sooner, he explained that he had a family emergency involving his parents and had to fly to the East Coast to attend to it. Was she still interested in getting together? She said yes and they did. They have been together ever since.

Her experience is one we all share. In the absence of direct knowledge or experience, the mind will fill in the blanks. I call this action *filling in the world*. When faced with an unknown, the mind fills it with what is already known. We draw from our pool of past knowledge, experience and belief to make sense of our present experience. This works in our favor when memory and future prediction support our survival or provide appropriate general guidelines for behavior.

The downside is that when it comes to making more subtle decisions, we rely on information that is inaccurate or out of context and represents old conclusions elevated to the position of belief. Instead of allowing the present moment to find new evidence from which to adjust old beliefs or generate new ones, we become subject to old patterns of interpretation that overlay our current experience and dominate our perception.

My friend was the victim of her own past conclusions about herself and others projected onto her current circumstance. The conditioned mind is not discerning enough to make the distinction between then and now. It operates by using association. If it looks enough like it, it must be it.

She created her own depression and anguish by accepting her inner narrative and out-picturing process as true and accurate. Her feelings, given what she believed to be true, were appropriate. She felt disappointment and grief for losing something she wanted. But the story she accepted as true was actually fiction masquerading as fact, and she used those feelings to support and justify the fiction. If she thought it and felt it, it must be true.

SUFFERING OURSELVES

After forty years as a psychotherapist, I can easily say that most of our suffering is self-generated and self-inflicted. This is why I try to practice the third skill: releasing myself from the fiction of the mind. I do not expect to rid myself of a natural function of the conscious mind. I simply want to release myself from its conditioned actions on my state of being. Becoming self-aware and conscious of how the mind works in generating my state of being, I can move from being reactive to a more responsive posture appropriate to the moment.

In the last chapter I described what happens when our story becomes unconscious. One consequence was that by denying authorship, we deny responsibility. We diminish the possibility for accurate feedback regarding our own creation. We fill in the world with ourselves, as my friend did, and masquerade it as something outside of ourselves, thus diminishing our self-awareness and new possibilities.

When I began to really listen to my own stories with genuine interest instead of aversion, they became a rich source of information about my psychology and how I had organized myself into being. I began taking back from the world the self I had projected onto it and to make progress with the dilemma I had set out to resolve: I don't exist *in* the world; the world exists *within* me. The world I knew as real, solid and physical was only a product of a creative act of perception, whose genesis lay beyond the outward manifestation of appearance.

The more these inner narratives and out-pictured images remain unexamined, the more we become subject to their impact. I discovered that bringing awareness to them, without trying to change their content, educated me about their role in generating my state of being. The more I understood the mechanics, the more I released myself from their form of fiction. Indeed, once viewed as fiction, I was able to see through the illusion of truth and realness I had assigned to them and recognize that these stories were my creations; I had chosen to embrace them as a way of resolving the dilemmas inherent in the interface between myself and the world. This awareness placed me in the center of the action as an active participant instead of sidelining me as a passive recipient of the thoughts, feelings and perceptions that informed my reactions.

These observations reinforced my revelatory experience in Hawaii with the current: *All my resignation comes from thinking, conceiving and ultimately perceiving that reality is real and fixed. I am never resigned in areas of my life where I understand and accept that what I see as real has only been assigned there by myself.*

The following is an example of an unowned story from my childhood. When I was young, I was very afraid to get in front of the class to give presentations. I was very self-conscious and afraid of people's judgments of my performance. When I was in the 6th grade I even made up a story that my mother was in the hospital with a broken arm to get out of having to give a book report in front of the class. The following day after not showing up to give the book report, I told the teacher that I was at the hospital with my mother, who had broken her arm from a fall, and that's why I missed class.

While this form of self-consciousness is common with children and adolescents, my fear was being projected onto those around me. I wasn't old enough or self-aware enough to recognize that I had a story about my audience, not the other way around. I expected them to be critical and judgmental of me. I had assigned my own view of myself onto my audience, and had made them the carriers of the feelings about me that I was unwilling to accept and acknowledge.

It was only when I became a young man, while giving a talk to a large group about a project I was involved in, that I resolved this issue for myself. On this occasion, while standing up to speak with the anxiety I normally felt, I hesitated and looked directly at my audience. I made eye contact with them and actually saw them separate from my projected story about them. They were there to hear me speak about something they were interested in, not to judge and humiliate me. Since that experience, whenever I speak in public, I remind myself that my audience is for me and wants to hear for themselves what I have to say.

As I continued exploring the mind and the body's dynamic relationship, I became aware of two major energy movements that represented their dynamic relationship and contributed to impacting my state of being in the moment. If I was going to manage my state through awareness rather than alter, change or correct my psychology, I had to learn to join in these movements as a way of consciously redirecting their impact on me. I call these movements—*expansion and contraction* and *hold and release* – the subjects of the next few chapters.

CHAPTER 20

EXPANSION AND CONTRACTION

WE ARE ALWAYS CHANGING SHAPE

Each of us is an intelligent and aware system of energy that is moved by meaning and evoked into being by an act of perception. From the vantage point of the field of energy and awareness that precedes the mind and body, we appear to continuously contract and expand. This motion of *contraction and expansion* represents our state of being moment to moment, and registers the actions taking place within and between the many parts that make us whole.

Each of us, in our own way, experiences this fact. We are beings who are in constant flux and change. While we are always looking to secure a sense of stability and safety outside ourselves, we often find that we are at the effect of our inside experience.

We experience this inner movement of expansion and contraction as feeling open or closed down, feeling good or feeling bad, feeling up or feeling down. We most often catch this action when responding to the events and circumstance we encounter in daily life. When we have a success at work, when a friend acknowledges what we mean to them, or when we stand in the face of nature's beauty, we feel ourselves expand. When we encounter frustration, criticism or pain, we contract, as if by reducing our presence and holding still leads us to safety and equanimity. However, seen from the field of energy and awareness beyond the mind/body, this movement of expansion and contraction is in constant flux as it responds to and reflects each moment of experience.

We often feel we have no control over this movement between expansion and contraction and therefore suffer from its motion. We mistake it for a psychological defect on our part, a lack of personal control or development, or a flaw in our personality. This misconception about why we don't feel more stability within ourselves ignores our basic nature; we are energy in motion.

We are constantly engaged with this energetic movement and attempt to manage it as we go through our day by trying to correct and control our thoughts and feelings, or by manipulating our outer environment. Our *relationship* with this movement determines the quality of our state of being in any moment. Do we resist it or act it out, or do we accept the movement it generates?

We normally engage with this movement by trying to manipulate its content. We focus on *what* we are experiencing instead of *how* we are organizing ourselves while we are experiencing. Generally, this results in us becoming identified with the content of our experience, and therefore at its effect. We feel victimized and powerless to move and initiate action within this space we take to be ourselves.

Instead, it is more helpful to realize that this movement is a direct result of perception and the meaning we have assigned to the present moment of experience. The field of energy and awareness that lies just outside our normal awareness is so attuned and responsive to the meaning we generate in each moment that it is never still. It creates the subtle moods and feelings that characterize our changing state of being. Our ability to accept the shifting energies that are a natural consequence of being an active perceiver is an important skill in managing our state of being.

CATCHING MYSELF IN MOTION

The following is a clear example of expansion and contraction. It is the kind of story that surfaces around the question –Where were you when?

Mendocino, California is a small town nestled on a headland overlooking the Pacific Ocean, backed by deep-forested coastal mountains. After the whaling and timber industries established the town in the late 1800's, it eventually morphed into a great meeting ground for hippie activity throughout the 60's and 70's until finally coming to rest as a picturesque tourist and art community. The Mendocino Art Center is a large complex of buildings occupying the northwest corner of the town proper.

In 2001, Ellen and I applied and were accepted as artists in residence for a year. I was now an accomplished ceramicist and Ellen a highly original painter. Being an artist in residence meant that we had a small one-bedroom apartment at the art center with complete access to studio space. Our only requirement was a little teaching and a commitment to create a body of work that would be shown at year's end in the Center's art gallery. This left us free to continue living part time in Palo Alto, California, about four hours down the coast below San Francisco, and also spend long periods of time at the Art Center.

Very early one morning in September I was in the studio finishing a piece of sculpture I had been working on for weeks. I looked out one of the large windows that ran the entire length of the studio. It was a glorious day. The sun was out and the sky was clear and bright. There was a slight breeze with a bite to it that let you know you were near the ocean. I decided to stop working and asked Ellen if she wanted to take a walk.

As I passed through the courtyard that separated the studio from our apartment, I saw a small group of people standing in a circle around a radio. I approached them and asked, "What's up?" Someone said, "Just listen." It was the morning of September 11, 2001. The first tower had come down and the second one was falling.

My first reaction was shock and disorientation, a kind of confusion when belief is suspended and no other interpretation fills the void. I felt like I was losing my ground. This was replaced by a strange sense of vulnerability that quickly morphed into fear and apprehension. As if my system would not tolerate this contraction, I immediately felt angry and aggressive. Each feeling had its own inner narrative that justified its presence: What the hell is happening? Am I safe? How does this affect me? Those bastards! They'll pay for this! All of this happened quickly as I stood there listening. I watched the same process go on with others who were standing around me.

After listening to the radio for another twenty minutes and feeling all my different emotional reactions, I decided to find Ellen and take our walk. After we had walked for about half an hour, sharing our reactions about the event, I experienced a moment where I shifted my attention away from all the thoughts and feelings, and instead looked outside of my reaction. I saw that the day was still beautiful, sunny and bright. The juxtaposition between my inside experience and my outside perception broke the trance-like state I was in. Wait a minute! I am not in New York experiencing this horror. This isn't happening to me in this moment. I am reacting as if it's personal and happening to me. I was already taking sides and beginning to walk down a path of hate and aggression that characterized the motives that sourced the act in the first place.

I then felt a release and was immediately flushed with sadness and compassion for everyone involved in the event, the victims as well as the attackers. Ellen and I gathered our things together so we could drive home to Palo Alto and be present for family, friends and clients. The world was about to change and I wanted to help where it touched me directly.

I am writing this chapter on September 11, 2011, and the national response to the 10th anniversary is loud and pervasive. After ten years we are still processing our response to 9/11 and being affected by the national policies that grew out of that response. My memory of how I responded that morning is vivid and was an important moment for me in recognizing how far I had come in my work with myself over the preceding years. I am sharing this with you because it has within it all of the ingredients that make the ability to manage one's state of being so important. Attention, thoughts, feelings and our sensory experience cooperate to provide the action that results in our perceived state of being. Our ability to use them constructively, and in the service of our highest intent, is the art of being self-aware.

If you could have seen my energy field throughout my experience on 9/11, you would have seen me expand into the bright sunny day, contract into fear and apprehension, try to expand through anger, and finally expand again after releasing the fear that had initially fueled my aggressive posture. Each movement was initiated by the interplay of thought and feeling in order to make sense of the unfolding circumstance. Only when I gave direct attention to my physical surroundings did I recognize where I was, and that it was my own filling in the world that had inspired all of this movement.

What initiates this movement between polarities? It is our perception; it is our interpretation of what is. There are two essential ingredients needed for this movement to occur: what we perceive as real in any moment; and what we perceive as present in any moment.

WHAT'S REAL AND WHAT'S PRESENT?

There is a wondrous aspect to our experience that goes unnoticed as we engage in normal everyday life. The physical body, and the emotional energy field that interfaces with it, do not recognize the difference between a thought about something and the actual presence of that something. I can evoke a loving feeling by *thinking* about my grandchildren just as well as if they were physically present. I can also evoke angry feelings in myself by thinking about how someone mistreated me three weeks ago, as if it were happening in this moment. I can become anxious right now thinking about a presentation I will be giving to two hundred people next month.

The mechanism that releases emotional energy throughout the physical body does not distinguish between a symbolic representation of a thing and the thing itself occurring in real time. Time and substance have no meaning; there is no difference between real or imagined events, between what we see and what we think or imagine. We are far more at the effect of our own perception than anything else.

Simply put, feeling follows thought. When I give my attention to listening to my inner narrative and out-picturing process, I am also calling forth all of the associated emotions surrounding them. Feelings are as conditioned as thought is. This is important to recognize because feeling is often used to justify the truth of our stories and facilitates our identification with them. On 9/11 my initial fear and aggressive feelings only served to support my story that I was the one threatened and therefore needed to fight back. In fact, in my direct experience, I was only standing there on a sunny morning listening to a report on the radio of a tragedy happening thousands of miles away. When supported by our feelings, our stories then become objective truth instead of being owned as the truth of our experience in the moment. When this occurs, self-awareness is diminished and conscious choice is reduced.

When we recognize that our story is fiction instead of fact, we are released from the impact it has on us in the moment. Only when we have released ourselves from this movement are we free to compassionately connect with those suffering the event.

When we bring our interest and attention to managing our state of being in the *moment*, instead of negotiating our image of our self through time, our suffering diminishes and our perception expands.

Notice for yourself how you expand and contract like a balloon either filled with air or deflated when feeling happy and joyful, feeling sad and depressed, feeling loved, feeling powerless or criticized, feeling empowered when you have gone beyond your current boundaries. I didn't initially understand that this movement is a natural consequence of how the mind and body interface until I began to observe their interdependence, and the energy and movement they create. Once I did, I began to enter into their dance as a cooperative partner, and to have more conscious choice about where this movement was taking me.

CHAPTER 21

ENERGY FOLLOWS THOUGHT

FEELING GOOD AND FEELING BAD

As I observed this movement of contraction and expansion, I was surprised to discover that I not only resisted the movement toward contraction in myself, but also the movement toward expansion. I knew I didn't like feeling bad, but I was surprised to discover that I also had a resistance to feeling too good. It was as if I had staked out the middle section of this continuum as a place where I could live and protect myself from the experience of too much of either. I felt that if I didn't monitor the movement of these energies, I might lose control and be swept away into dangerous waters.

Once I became clear that thought and feeling were automatically connected, I started to disconnect them by listening for the inner narratives that accompany certain feelings. For instance, when I had a disagreement with my mate and felt frustrated or angry, I could hear my narratives the clearest.

I know this sounds as if it would be more difficult. It wasn't. Where my feelings were the strongest, so was the voice in my head telling me why I was justified in feeling as I did. Once my feelings began to move and dissipate, I could still hear my narrative encouraging me to hold on to them. As I would walk around muttering inside myself about the circumstance, I was able to observe how these two separate parts of my experience supported each other in delivering a fiction that I accepted as a fact.

After separating them, I examined their validity and relevance to the current circumstance that had evoked them. I felt safe to explore their relationship and to allow the movement into contraction or expansion without turning to resistance as a form of control. Joining with the movement, and following its direction actually allowed me more control.

I have learned that feeling good is the product of treating all feeling with equanimity. When you feel bad, feel bad; when you feel good, feel good; embrace either feeling with presence and authenticity without grasping, holding or resisting its movement through you.

I have also learned that most of us are not committed to being happy or feeling good. Instead, we are committed to reversing bad feelings so that we can start to feel good again. This leads us to correcting ourselves in a way that keeps us struggling, like a fly on the spider's web: struggle and you are caught. Instead, self-acceptance and stillness provide the way out.

Feelings are energy in movement; they are not capricious. Sensations, feelings and emotional content follow thought (our inner narrative) to complete and construct our immediate felt experience of the moment. When we are conscious that we are listening to an inner conversation or viewing pictures, can we be aware of any sensations or feelings that are also present? In other words, does our mood shift and move in relationship to our inner dialogue or subjective viewing? When we have angry, happy or sad feelings, can we experience the relationship between what we see or hear inside and what we feel in the body? If feelings accompany our pictures and inner conversation, are they used to justify or make more real the story that is being entertained? Do we use our feelings to validate our thoughts?

Contraction and expansion create an energetic force that acts upon us and, at the same time, is initiated by us. *The very act of perceiving alters the shape and texture of the perceiver and the perceived.* Simply by being ourselves, we are also acting upon ourselves. This awareness represents a shift in consciousness and a further release from the fiction of the mind. Instead of just investigating and observing the dance between our ideas and our feelings, we can participate more proactively in the interaction. Ideas and feelings are energetic objects that can be played with to produce a desired result in being. They are not sacred, nor do they belong to the essential self. Instead, they are tools of creation, ready and waiting to be utilized by the self.

As I continued to explore this domain, I realized that I had always been free to use these tools creatively, and was doing so all the time, only unconsciously. Until I understood the mechanics of my experience, and the relationships of the parts to the whole, I was at the effect of these movements. With conscious awareness, I now had the opportunity to participate more fully in the direction my experience took instead of being in reaction to it. As I monitored and tuned into the energetic movement of contraction and expansion, the attachment to my stories reduced and altered. I began to resonate with the fact of the body and thus be released from the fiction of the mind.

As we go through our day, we are always expanding and contracting, experiencing subtle shifts in perception, sensation and feeling that shape our state of being. We fill in the world with our story and we respond to this creative act of perception as if we are innocent of its source. However, when we participate in this action with awareness, we experience a shift in consciousness and are no longer at the effect of our own creation. We can choose to direct its unfolding with new creativity in the service of our highest intention.

BECOMING NORMAL

I began to experience a newfound freedom to allow the contracting and expanding energy to occur without interpreting these shifts as if they were symptomatic of a personal flaw, or of an inability to control my reactions to life as I encountered it. I discovered I am normal. I just hadn't understood what normal meant on a deeper level. Normal is a state of being where the perceiver and perceived appear to be separate, but are in fact one continuous field of meaning and energy. Knowing that I was subject to the natural dynamic of mind and body generated in me a profound acceptance of, and compassion for, myself as a human being.

Observing my own contraction and expansion gave me a new platform from which to explore my nature with curiosity and genuine interest. I could know myself beyond the need to rescue my self from myself. I was now free to play with my nature instead of always being in reaction to it. The natural contractions and expansions of my energy became a guide to organizing myself into being.

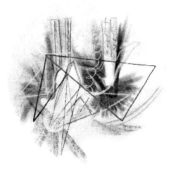

CHAPTER 22

HOLD AND RELEASE

CONCEPTUAL GRAVITY

While enjoying this new acceptance of allowing myself to contract and expand in the moment, I became aware of another movement, subtle and less visible, but just as powerful in shaping the quality of my experience. I call this movement *hold and release*. As seen from the field of energy and awareness within which the mind and body rest, hold and release is a powerful and subtle force behind the movement of contraction and expansion. It is more enduring than the spontaneous expanding and contracting that naturally occurs in response to a moment of perception. Hold and release is the result of a fixation and identification with the *content* of our experience in lieu of experiencing the present moment. Taking ourselves to be the thoughts, feelings and body sensations of our surface experience, we fail to recognize that our essential

167

identity is in the ever present field of awareness that surrounds and contains them.

We hold ourselves fixed, through time, in the form of the stories we tell ourselves about our experience. We are held to the self we know, always returning to the familiar experience of ourselves with its characteristic feelings, thoughts and points of view.

We are, however, released from the familiar during these moments of intuitive knowing, insight, vision, inspiration and revelation that transform our experience to a new level of perception. The boundaries imposed on us by these familiar stories dissolve, and we are shown new possibilities for expanded awareness, thought, feeling and action. We are always in the process of being both held in place by our self-identification *and* being released into newness from the source beyond the conscious self. This is the movement of being and becoming in action.

Hold and release is set in motion by the presence of what I call *conceptual gravity*. Just as physical gravity draws the objects in its field to ground, so conceptual gravity draws our awareness to a baseline consciousness (vibration or feeling) that we habitually move toward and come to rest in. When we are not conscious and active in choosing our state in the moment, we are pulled toward a *baseline frequency*. This pull is our unexamined beliefs. Its contents are the trains of thought and associated feelings, bodily sensations and points of view that we experience and take to be our familiar self. It is a *sensed feeling state* to which we are drawn over and over again.

OUR BASELINE FREQUENCY

The concept of baseline frequency is an energetic way of identifying the form and shape of the conditioned self and bringing it into fuller awareness and acceptance. Our baseline frequency is that feeling state toward which we naturally gravitate. It is where we land when we are not being self-aware. When we say, "That's just who I am" or after an emotional upheaval or illness, we declare "I feel myself again," we are referring to this baseline, the subjective feeling tone we identify as normal for ourselves. Our baseline frequency is a felt sense generated from the inside. It becomes the touchstone we always return to as a natural consequence of living in the pull of conceptual gravity.

Our beliefs underlie and support our baseline frequency. These beliefs exist as narratives or clusters of stories that surround and give validity to our unique baseline consciousness. They constitute the field of meaning, the lens through which we interpret reality.

For example, feeling underappreciated by those around me is a feeling that can pull me to my baseline. When I stop and feel this feeling in my body, it turns into a sad story about how people are indifferent to me, and don't understand me. If I continue to listen to these voices, they take me back to my early experiences as a child, when both parents worked and gave me little attention. The conclusion I arrived at then and which I assigned to my baseline, was the belief that people around me will not make the effort to know me as I know myself. This belief about the nature of reality continues to support my feeling of sadness and becomes part of the conceptual energy that holds me to this baseline frequency.

Our experience is always moving and in flux. An idea comes into our consciousness and passes away. A feeling moves through the body and is replaced by another. Obsessive thoughts, protracted emotional feelings or physical discomfort, if observed closely, show evidence of movement and change. Even our experience of circumstance (the world) is subject to the constant fluctuations of our perceptions of it.

However, the one aspect of our experience that resists this natural movement is the *stories* we tell ourselves about our selves or about the world. These stories persist through time and escape the impact of our on-going, immediate, direct experience. They carry the frozen decisions of the past. When elevated to the status of a belief, these stories become conclusions we are not willing to submit to direct experience, hence they resist moving and changing. They constitute the building blocks for baseline consciousness, the experience of self that is automatic, reactive and absent of conscious choice. In this way, we trade our aliveness, freedom and responsiveness for the constancy, predictability and security of our baseline frequency. We get what we focus on. We try to avoid suffering by defaulting to the content that generated the suffering in the first place. We remain embedded in our normal baseline consciousness. We seek the self we know and expect it to produce the self we aspire to be.

These beliefs, appearing in the form of narratives, cluster at our baseline, and hold us in place. They are part of the conceptual field of gravity that pulls us down to the ground of being we are willing to accept as our familiar self. This process of identifying with a fixed position about reality creates the narratives that dominate our internal listening, and separates us from the voice of wisdom and compassion that exists beyond the frequencies of our baseline consciousness.

Our stories tend to dominate our experience when we are feeling most insecure. It would be more effective, however, to practice awareness and compassion for ourselves. Then our frozen choices can be melted and released back into the energy of immediate, direct experience. In this way our baseline consciousness can become fluid, open and responsive and no longer an obstruction to new experience and expanded consciousness.

A quick way to make baseline more visible to yourself is to identify a feeling you carry or revisit with some regularity, stop the feeling in its tracks, feel it, and become present to it. As you do this, listen for the voices that are connected to it and the story they weave to justify feeling the way you do. The core belief will be hiding in the story as justification for the feeling. I give some practices in Part Four of this book to help make beliefs more visible and to check their accuracy in reflecting the experience of the current self.

Our baseline represents the vibrational field and creative environment used by the deeper self to plant new seeds that grow into new conceptions about the nature of our perceived reality. The deeper wisdom of the self must speak through this atmosphere to inform and evolve the conscious self. If the conscious mind is too rigid in its interpretation of reality, the deeper self and its wisdom will not be readily heard or taken advantage of. Our baseline consciousness represents the degree of receptivity we experience in discerning that new vision, inspiration or revelation provided by the inner self as it raises the frequency and energetic value of the conscious self.

Underlying our experience of baseline consciousness is our interface with the unknown. Here the self is committed to seeking fulfillment instead of satisfaction, novelty over the familiar and meaning in place of constancy. Its job is to provide the inspiration that funds new creativity and provides the infusion of energy that supports the ever-evolving nature of our being. Its aim is to move us forward instead of holding us in place. Its method is revelation. It brings sight to what has not been seen and provides vision past where we are currently held in place.

CHAPTER 23

PLAYING WITH RELEASE

CHOOSE TO FEEL GOOD

We are extraordinary beings inhabiting the ordinary circumstances of our lives. To find the extraordinary, we must look through the personality and the baseline frequency it occupies. If we keep looking at the personality as something to fix instead of a unique set of possibilities to be realized, the extraordinary being that we are will be obscured from sight.

The answer to this conundrum is to realize that we are beings who have the capacity to generate our experience and to be subject to it simultaneously. We are the cause and effect of ourselves. Because of this, we have the inherent capacity to elevate the frequency of our state of being at will. *We can feel good by choice.*

As I played with the movement of hold and release and became aware of what held me to my baseline, I began to focus on the release aspect of this movement. My intention was to release myself from the fiction of the mind, not to challenge or change my conditioned self. I wanted to hold the self I knew in awareness while I looked *through* it to elevate my baseline to a higher frequency. I wanted to co-operate with my experience, not challenge it to resist my efforts. I discovered that I can achieve this release in three ways:

1. I can play with the images and pictures the mind produces and move them to a higher frequency.

2. I can bypass the mind and go directly to the current of energy that supports the form I choose to take.

3. I can listen through my conditioned narratives to hear the deeper voice of wisdom that resides just under my everyday consciousness.

When I explore the first option with students, I ask them to choose to feel good right now. If they are able to, I ask them how they achieved it. Universally, everyone reports that holding a positive or pleasurable thought leads to a positive feeling. This is what we have learned to do to feel good. For example, when I call up an image of playing with one of my grandchildren, I feel joyous and warm all over. When I think about having finished this book, I feel content and fulfilled. These examples represent our inherent understanding of how the mind and body cooperate to produce our experience.

The downside of this method, of course, is its opposite. We can choose to feel bad by evoking images that contract us. Feelings of fear, hurt and disappointment always follow their corresponding images in the mind.

However, when we bring conscious awareness to this process, we can learn to play with the images themselves, and evolve our baseline frequency to become a more constant source of positive support.

It is difficult to be old and new at the same time; we all wish we could stay the same while changing in ways we desire. This is a perfect formula for getting stuck. As I enjoyed more release from the fiction of the mind, I saw that focusing on *changing* my old images and beliefs only energized them and reinforced their presence.

In others words, attempting to fix and correct an already concretized idea only reinforces the conceptual gravity of our baseline frequency. Attention grants beingness, whether it's positive or negative attention.

REPLACE THE OLD WITH THE NEW

To become who we wish to be, we have to let go of old images and adopt new ones. This process often occurs so smoothly that we don't recognize how an old idea or point of view has been replaced with a new one that is more aligned with our current experience. We think that the old image or belief has changed into the new one.

In the short course I offer in Part Four, I provide a process for uncovering our beliefs at baseline and a method for replacing them with more constructive images. Once we uncover our attachment to old images that no longer reflect our current experience, we can hold these images in awareness with equanimity. This releases us from the conceptual gravity they have contributed to, and elevates our baseline frequency.

CONNECTING TO THE CURRENT

The second way to facilitate release is to bypass the mind and go directly to the field of energy that contains the mind and body. This current is a constant source of positive feeling and is always accessible. Just as the mind is always present and can be accessed through thoughts and images, this current of felt energy can always be found: in and through the body, first as sensation, and second as a felt sense of the field of energy the body rests within. It exists independent of our interpretations and does not rely on any preconceived image to call it forth. It belongs to our spirit and is always available.

We can connect with this current of energy through sensation. If we shift our attention into body sensation and drop into a relaxed, settled state, this experience will deepen into a sense of energy flowing through the body. From this felt sense, we can use our will to call forth a specific feeling to appear and spread throughout the body.

It is fascinating to me that we know so little about this incredible source of wellbeing, which is so close in awareness and has no obstacles to its access except knowing it's there and making the choice to connect with it. Once this feeling is called upon, the conscious mind will then begin to receive images and narratives that the energy brings with it, one's that represent the source of the current itself.

When we release ourselves into this current, its energy floods our system with light and rarefied frequencies that begin to elevate our baseline consciousness. This is why the practice of meditation is so effective over time. If we continue to experience an elevated state with some consistency, it begins to change the resonance of all parts of our system.

THE QUIET VOICE WITHIN

The third form of release from the conceptual gravity that holds us to our baseline frequency is developing a deeper inner listening. Just under our baseline frequency is another layer of knowing that speaks with a different voice, sharing its wisdom in a quiet way that vibrates with acceptance, precognition, energy and intelligence. When we listen for this voice, it moves forward into conscious awareness. It follows the principle that what we give our attention to takes the foreground in our perceptual field.

I have asked students over the years to describe the difference between their intuitive voice and their conditioned voice. Their responses typically fall into the following categories.

Characteristics of the *conditioned* voice:
Encourages delay and procrastination
Encourages distraction
Evokes caution through anxiety and fear
Maintains and protects the status quo
Encourages reactive feelings
Seeks drama as a means of vitality
Judges and compares to establish a sense of identity
Wants to fix or compensate for the lack of something

Characteristics of the *intuitive* voice:

Motivates and encourages

Guides and informs

Reflects and supports our deepest desires

Illuminates the unseen; brings light to what is obscure

Accepts *what is* without judgment

Provides possibilities for action

Inspires and energizes

In addition to elevating the frequency of our baseline, developing an inner listening evokes the emergence of this inherent voice of wisdom for us and brings it to conscious awareness. We start to hear and see the wisdom and guidance that is always going on just beneath our normal perception instead of the drama and suffering of the conditioned mind.

This is a radical shift in consciousness. You get what you focus on. Typically, we keep ourselves embedded in normal consciousness out of an attempt to avoid suffering. When we are able to distinguish between the stream of narrative representing our conditioned images from the stream of inner support of the quiet voice within, our baseline frequency begins to shift.

This inner wisdom is such an intimate part of us that we often do not notice it and, therefore, do not avail ourselves of its usefulness. The reactive mind is so loud and urgent that it captures our attention; its conversation is cautious, fearful and protective, and has a different tone than the quiet voice within. The quiet voice is open, safe, experimental and playful. It is easy to ignore because it doesn't consume time or energy by focusing on the past or future; it only concerns itself with the now. It speaks to us of possibilities and experiments, of joy and fullness, of delights and safety. It doesn't tell us what to do; it shows us how to go about what we want to do. We are informed of the method and direction of pursuing our heart's desire.

When this voice is distinguished and brought into conscious awareness, listened for and engaged with, the movement of hold and release shifts us to a new level of vibration. The movement resonates at a higher octave, repeating its invitation to expand even further. This is the way we grow and evolve. We create boundaries of identity and live within them until the need to transcend our own creation becomes evident. Then we let go of our holding, and step into new forms of release.

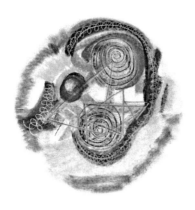

CHAPTER 24

FALLING INTO ALIGNMENT

BECOMING A PROACTIVE BEING

I have been sharing the possibilities that exist for us to learn about ourselves from our selves. We are a miraculous construction; we have been granted a wonderful gift as part of our nature, the ability to be self-aware. From the very act of being ourselves, we learn not only about our own particular nature, but also the nature we all share, our human nature. We can do this consciously, by choice, as an act of will.

Our capacity for self-awareness sets the stage for a unique opportunity. It provides the means by which we release ourselves from being the actor who is acted upon and instead become the actor who participates in constructing his or her own life. We can enter the moment not as a reactive being, whose stance is organized to take and receive, but as a proactive being, whose stance is organized to bring and give. On the one hand, we take life too seriously, and on the other, we do not take playful existence seriously enough. When we fall into alignment through skillful self-awareness, our experience takes on the energy of play and creativity in the service of learning about our selves and the reality we create.

Just as we manipulate objects in the objective world, we can also manipulate ideas and feelings in our subjective world. Creation originates from the inside and appears as things, events and objects on the outside. Our experience in each moment represents a living picture that is projected from the inside of our consciousness to the outside. We then meet and interact with our picture as if it is real and substantial, validated by our outer senses. We evolve ourselves by playing with our creations and generating new possibilities out of our own experience. We are always meeting ourselves as the world. We grow, evolve and expand as a result. This is a profoundly intelligent process that is self-generated and is always supporting the growth of the perceiver.

When we revisit our definition of self-awareness—having conscious knowledge of our nature and the uniting principles that underlie our subjective experience—we start to realize its meaning. By emphasizing three primary skills throughout this book; taking control of one's attention, grounding oneself in the fact of the body, and releasing oneself from the fiction of the mind, we have explored their usefulness in generating conscious knowledge about our nature and, in the process, have uncovered many patterns and relationships that together generate the form and quality our subjective experience takes.

These three skills represent a specific, conscious process we can use to move us toward deeper self-awareness. When we practice them, we gain access to our feelings, thoughts, and intuitive promptings, as well as to higher energy states that bring a sense of grace, calm, and insight to our behavior, choices, and performance within the circumstances of our life.

Something happens when we bring our full attention to the moment of present experience. The world of our outer perception becomes brighter; our thinking becomes clearer, and our feelings become more vivid and, paradoxically, more subject to our choice. This is the first level of magic the moment holds for us, and is the start of taking control of our attention and exercising our capacity to choose our focus as an act of will. This alignment results in the state of being self-aware.

As we allow the moment to deepen and expand, we discover that it contains multiple layers of magic that can inform, enrich, heal and enlighten our everyday experience. Not only does the personal aspect of who we are become more available, but so do those dimensions of the self that are invisible to normal perception. They become apparent and available for creative use in constructing the reality we wish to experience.

When we rely on self-image to create our sense of self, we see only a representation of ourself that we have constructed over time, and it reduces our freedom to process experience directly. We are then stuck with trying to get our experience to match our image instead of using direct experience to generate a new and accurate picture of who we are. When we release our attachment to self-image, our center of perception shifts to a more balanced state where sensory, intuitive, mental and energetic faculties become a valid source for producing our perception of reality.

FALLING INTO ALIGNMENT

As we deepen our self-awareness, we become more sensitive to the energetic movements and information available at more subtle levels of consciousness. When we are able to shift attention from thinking (mind) to sensation (body) to sensing (energy), our perception expands into a multidimensional view of the self that sources information inaccessible to the mind alone.

When thinking, sensation and sensing are joined they produce a more comprehensive experience of self and a larger field of experience, observation, and awareness. When our thought process, our body of sensations and feelings, and energetic experiences are brought into *alignment,* we are then able to receive them as a cooperative process, which is unifying and perceptually integrated.

This alignment creates a new vantage point from which to discover and make visible the creative relationship between these otherwise discrete aspects of self-experience. A new foundation for skillfully managing our state of being is born.

As the energy movements we are normally subject to become increasingly visible, we are more conscious of the perceptual cues that indicate whether our state of being is contracting or expanding. Our ability to identify the source of this movement is enhanced, permitting us to accept and receive our contraction or expansion with equanimity, seeing through our judgments of either being right or wrong. Our ability to now differentiate between direct sensory experience and symbolic experience supports this movement, and releases us from the grip of memories or projections of the future.

Consequently, we can choose to inhabit a more present state of awareness, which is attuned to the moment of emerging experience.

As we give greater attention to managing our state of being, suffering diminishes and perception expands. When experience is perceived as meaningful and intelligent, we see that our state of being is a cooperative venture. And if we are positioned properly within the self, observation and direct knowing reveal the intelligent patterns of meaning and creativity that are the foundation of self-awareness.

CHAPTER 25

ENTERING INTO ATTUNEMENT WITH YOUR LARGER SELF

A NEW COOPERATIVE PRESENCE

I f we practice the three skills outlined in this book with some degree of diligence, we can produce the experience of feeling centered and present to the flow of our ongoing experience. We can inhabit our essence and receive our thoughts, feelings, sensations and energetic knowing with greater skill. We are able to look out into the physical world and into the subjective world with equal grace and distinction. We are no longer at odds with the different parts of the self, and we can hold all parts in awareness, knowing how they cooperate to produce the self we know.

This new positioning sets us up to move into *attunement* with the energies of our larger consciousness. We can begin to play creatively with these energies and learn about our selves from ourselves in a new way. Instead of only using our skills to achieve balance and equanimity, we can develop a cooperative relationship with the source of vision, intuition, and inspiration that lies just beneath our everyday consciousness. Bringing this relationship into conscious awareness establishes a new, cooperative presence that guides and informs us as we go about our lives.

ALTERNATE FOCUS

Our attention and awareness is not always focused on what is familiar. When we observe ourselves carefully, we see that we are like a flickering light. One moment our attention is here, and in the next moment it is somewhere else. This shifting of focus is a natural function of ordinary consciousness.

The most dramatic illustration of this shift can be seen in the rhythm of wakefulness and sleep. Without sleep our reality comes apart, we go crazy and eventually will die. We cannot sustain our presence in the physical body and the physical world without this coming and going. This is what I mean when I describe human beings as committed visitors. We have committed ourselves to physical form, but we are not bound by this commitment. Our consciousness still retains the freedom to come and go, a movement that is crucial to our ability to remain present within the physical form itself.

Thus, our need for *alternate focus* is a natural by product of the ongoing shifts in consciousness, whether we are conscious of these shifts or not. They are part of the ground of being from which our present self draws its energy, inspiration and vitality.

Other common forms of alternate focus occur naturally throughout our day: musing, contemplation, daydreaming, night dreaming, trance states, meditation and those moments when we are infused with vision, inspiration and revelatory insight. When they occur, the conscious self is either being released from its concentration on its physical form, or the inner self is inserting new material into conscious awareness. The more we become skilled at discerning these alternate focus moments, the more we can take advantage of the information and creativity that are at the heart of the experience. This discernment provides the evidence that the conscious self is always seeking, i.e., that we are connected to a larger field of meaning and purpose.

There are two ways I learned to play with alternate focus. One is to practice a structured and conscious method for shifting to another focus, and exploring its possibilities for knowledge and experience. This is the skill of grounding in the fact of the body and shifting to the field of awareness and energy beyond it. All contemplative and meditative practices in the great spiritual traditions practice these shifts as a way of consciously connecting with a larger state of consciousness.

The second way is to discover and reveal the natural, seemingly random, occurrence of alternate focus within our daily life. When we practice both ways, we can bring them together as one unified experience. The secret to bringing these occurrences to conscious awareness is simple, and does not involve magic or mystery. It involves the principle of perception mentioned earlier: *What you give your attention to becomes foreground.*

Some common experiences that can alert us to these moments are:

Sudden calm

Relaxation

Warm energy

A rush of energy through the body

A sense of opening outward or expanding

Boundaries dissolving or changing

A feeling of expectancy

Feeling a new idea, vision or possibility being born

A feeling of safety

A feeling of connectedness and inclusiveness

New insight or perception around old or current circumstances

Acceptance of what is present without judgment

New possibilities for action not seen or contemplated before

When we recognize these shifts in frequency from our normal state, we can pay attention and cooperate with the potential they hold for a new experience, view or insight. Once we familiarize ourselves with these cues, we can ask for and expect a shift to occur. We can then grant it validity by choosing to hold it as real and ascribe it meaning.

LEVELS OF HARMONIC FREQUENCY

The following are some commonly experienced examples of alternate focus. I have added my own and other's subjective descriptions of knowledge and material that can consciously be evoked while inhabiting these particular harmonic frequencies. I use the term harmonic here to describe a vibratory frequency that must be present, either by practice or spontaneously, in order to allow entry into any of these states. These different levels of consciousness and frequency each represent a particular focus from which new viewpoints and perspectives can be derived.

Level One – This harmonic frequency is associated with normal, waking consciousness, when our attention is directed towards the external environment. This is the ego state where our focus is directed outward into the world of objectivity and substance, where everything is seen as object, even ourselves.

Level Two – This is a relaxed state where thinking is minimized and there is a pleasurable feeling of floating calm, and lucidity. This state of consciousness becomes foreground when we ground ourselves in the fact of the body, feel released from the mind, and enter the field of awareness and energy beyond the mind/body. It is also a layered experience; the first layer contains predominately current beliefs, ideas and associations. However, there are also mixed and interwoven associations that may be called self-unifying associations. These provide a unifying sense of psychic continuity and identity.

It is on this level that we experience the field of energy that precedes the mind/body. It contains those possibilities for development that are not sufficiently strong to be conscious to the ego. The harmonic of this level can be used for healing self and others. It also provides a great framework for creativity, concentration, refreshment, rest, problem solving and meditation. Some past life material can also be picked up from here.

Level Three – This harmonic frequency is associated with deep states of relaxation, advanced meditation practice, bursts of creative insight, twilight sleep learning and vivid mental imagery.

In this state one turns attention inward into deeper layers of consciousness, or outward to a new perception of alignment with the mind/body/world of our experience. In this state, information dealing with the soul's knowledge of itself can be received.

It is from this focus point that communication between the living and the dead may take place. Historical knowledge and verification of identity through time may also be achieved through communication with past life material. In fact, information about the world prior to the physical evolution of man is also available at this level. The history of plant and animal life and the evolution of the physical planet can be viewed. These various layers of consciousness represent a vast pool of archeological knowledge from which the present self may draw knowledge, psychic continuity and balance.

Level Four – This level of frequency is associated with a deep state of hypnosis and thought incubation. It is very close to sleep and therefore hard to maintain. I find this state to be the best channel for receiving revelatory information and radical new conceptions that are outside the box of my conscious mind.

COMING FULL CIRCLE

Within the familiar self lies a whole universe of knowledge and experience waiting to be revealed if we take the time to look. To learn about ourselves from our selves is at the heart of who we are and who we can be. If being self-aware is our nature and our essence, living in a state of self-awareness is our vision and promise. To inhabit our essence is to look out and look in with equal grace and discernment. When we can bring these two halves of ourselves together as a unified experience, we will have achieved a perceptual integration that supports our movement toward a more expanded state of being.

One morning many years ago in Hawaii, while sitting in the speaking experience the following statement was made. It is a good place to end this part of the book; circling back around to touch once more the energy and voice that inspired this writing:

"Let me say to you that you live as a multiplicity. When you find yourself wanting, desiring and yearning for a particular experience, it is because this is already present within your consciousness. You are not a singular entity from which wants appear and disappear at random in some meaningless and capricious manner. You play a vital role and service to a larger beingness of which you are a part. You are the creative element, the active ingredient in allowing creative qualities of consciousness to emerge into the particular reality that you represent. It is not just that you are graced by deeper aspects of your own nature, but that you have the opportunity to confer and give life within your own perception to aspects of the multiplicity of which I speak. In this sense, you are a fundamental giver of life within the particular reality you inhabit. When this is understood, it allows for a less personal focus than you normally hold as a psychological entity or structure fixed through time and space. It allows you the opportunity to experience a cooperative sense of being, so that you may be the giver and the given simultaneously. The joy of this relationship is complete, yet creative and ever expanding. It is the release of self to Self."

PART FOUR

SELF-AWARENESS
PRACTICES

WORKING WITH THE
THREE SKILLS

Throughout this book you have been discovering the process of becoming self-aware. In this last section, I invite you to participate in a short course of practices that will give you the opportunity to personalize the process and make it your own.

These incremental steps will give you the experience of working with the three skills described in this book. I encourage you to follow the steps in order since each skill builds upon the previous ones. Stay with a practice until you are comfortable with the experience it was created to produce, and then move on to the next practice. Of course, all of these practices can and should be returned to often so they become integrated into a new way of organizing yourself into being. Use the chapters in the book for reference as you proceed. Most importantly, keep it fun, and continue to support your curiosity by suspending judgment, embracing patience and acknowledging new experience.

SKILL ONE

TAKING CONTROL OF YOUR ATTENTION

THE SEVEN PRINCIPLES OF ATTENTION

These principles represent how we organize our experience to perceive the way we do. Taken together, they describe the natural structure that lies hidden within every act of perception. They are the meta-foundation that gives structure and meaning to our practice, and therefore are the best place to begin.

FIRST PRINCIPLE

ATTENTION IS FREE TO MOVE AND IS SUBJECT TO YOUR WILL. YOU CAN CHOOSE YOUR FOCUS IN ANY MOMENT.

All of the practices in this part of the book invite you to enter the moment proactively, and take responsibility for where you direct your attention. That is why choosing your focus is the starting point in the process of becoming self-aware; it rescues your attention from unconscious control. You can learn to arrive in the moment with your will and attention joined. When they are joined, it places you in the moment as actor instead of being acted upon. It is one of the many forms of presence we will practice.

PRACTICE 1

FOLLOWING THE MOVEMENT OF ATTENTION

Find a comfortable place where you can sit quietly without outside interruptions. Without imposing any form of concentration or focus, watch how your attention naturally moves on its own throughout your field of experience.

One moment you may be in thought, the next targeting some object in your outside environment, back to thought, then into feeling or sensation and back again. Let your attention circle and move on its own. Yes, you will hear a voice talking to you about what you are doing. This is just another thought attempting to track your progress, and will be the focus of your attention at times. Just observe and verify that attention moves on its own when not consciously directed by you.

PRACTICE 2

HOLDING FOCUS

Our first objective is to begin to bring attention under our control. This is done by an act of will; we can choose to focus and direct our attention. When we relinquish this choice, attention is moved unconsciously by habit and conditioning.

Find a comfortable place where you can sit quietly without outside interruptions.

1. For a minute or two at a time, take conscious control of where you direct your attention. Joining your attention with your sight, look at an object near you and hold your attention there as long as you can until attention reverts back to its automatic movement toward thought or some other focus.

2. Create an image in your mind of someone you care about and hold your attention there until the image changes or attention moves on to a different focus.

3. Lastly, direct your attention to feeling your feet on the floor, joining attention with sensation, and holding this focus until the propensity for attention to move takes over.

PRACTICE 3

ENLARGING YOUR FOCUS

The next time you go into a public place, like a restaurant or retail store, take a moment to see if you can expand your attention to encompass the whole room, with all of its diverse activity. Allow all of the activity to move on its own without choosing to focus on any one particular action.

PRACTICE 4

CONTROLLING MOVEMENT INTO AND AWAY FROM THOUGHT

1. While sitting with a friend in conversation, focus your attention on listening to their words without thinking internally about what the words mean to you or what your response should be.

2. Sitting quietly, let yourself drift into thought about how your day is going. When you recognize that you are in thought, shift your attention to a sensation in the body. Then shift your attention to an object in your immediate environment.

This practice is important because we tend to live in our thoughts, and confuse thinking about something with giving attention to something. When we consciously choose to shift attention away from thought, we can become aware of the difference between truly listening to what our friend is saying and thinking about our responses to what they are saying. Thought only happens in the mind, while attention is free to move throughout our entire field of perception. When we can control our attention's movement into and away from thought, we have taken a giant step in bringing our mind under conscious control. Instead of feeling at the effect of our thoughts, we can begin to use our thoughts to support our intentions with more grace.

SECOND PRINCIPLE

ATTENTION ALWAYS PLACES YOU AT THE CENTER OF YOUR EXPERIENCE. YOU ARE THE PERCEIVER UPON WHOM EXPERIENCE IMPRINTS ITSELF.

We are hardwired to rest in the middle of our experience. What we see, hear, smell, taste and touch is always registered by an unseen presence that occupies the moment of emerging experience. Experience arranges itself around and through an unseen awareness that is always present; attention moves out from and returns to this center point, giving us our deepest sense of identity and validity, no matter what form the experience takes. There are two ways attention establishes this center: by locating us in space and placing us in time.

PRACTICE 5

YOU ARE IN THE MIDDLE OF YOUR EXPERIENCE

You can do this practice standing, sitting or lying down. Bring your attention to the space occupied by your body, and sense your orientation within it. You will find yourself occupying a front, back, left, right, top and bottom orientation.

Now, feel how your awareness of being in the body rests in the middle of these sensed coordinates. What does it feel like?

This unseen orientation places you in the middle of a 360-degree field of awareness with you at its center, defining and creating your sense of immediacy and location in space, you being *here* as opposed to you being *there*. Whether in stillness or in movement, this center goes with you into every experience you encounter.

PRACTICE 6

YOUR SENSES ARE IN THE PRESENT MOMENT

Take a moment and join your attention with any of your five outer senses. In your immediate surroundings, look at, listen to, taste, touch or smell something near you.

Notice how all of these senses place you in the present, the immediate now.

PRACTICE 7

STEPPING INTO TIME.

Just as we find ourselves in the middle of space, orienting ourselves relative to top, bottom, left, right, front and back, so too we find ourselves in the middle of linear time with the present as our center resting between past and future. Our most immediate and intimate relationship with time is through this center we recognize as right *now*. There is no way to extract ourselves physically from the experience of now; we can only do this mentally.

While sitting quietly, let your attention roam throughout the room, taking in all the objects that occupy space within it. Then bring your attention back to how the body feels resting in your chair. Notice how the room and the objects within it, as well as your body sensations, have no past or future attached to them. They are present and in the moment.

Now let yourself drift into an earlier event that happened before you began this practice. What were you doing? Notice that you have to go into thought to create the past.

Now, sit and let yourself imagine what the rest of your day will be like. What experiences do you expect to encounter as your day unfolds? Notice where your attention goes to see this projected future.

These simple shifts in attention show us how, physically, we live in the present, between our mental conceptions of past and future. However, through the conscious control of our attention, we can step into and out of time at will. When we are attuned to the *physical* moment, we are resting in the center of time between past and future.

THIRD PRINCIPLE

ATTENTION BRIDGES SUBJECT AND OBJECT. YOU ARE SUBJECT; ALL OTHER IS OBJECT. ATTENTION ALLOWS US TO TRAVEL BETWEEN THE TWO.

Our ordinary everyday consciousness comes to us divided. We are both private and public simultaneously. Like a coin we have two sides; one side sees, the other side is seen. Although both sides are happening at the same time, we can only know the side of ourselves that sees, and the side of others that is seen, i.e., the inner half of ourselves, and the outer half of others. This is the way we normally perceive. Attention allows us to travel between public and private realities, holding them as two sides of a larger whole.

PRACTICE 8

CROSSING THE DIVIDE

Sit quietly and look at an object in the room. While looking at the object, allow yourself to have thoughts about it. Notice your attention shifting from looking at the object to the thoughts you are having about it.

Your attention is crossing two different worlds with ease. One we call physical, the object in the room. The other we experience as non-physical, your thoughts about the object.

Your thoughts represent your subjective experience and the object you are looking at represents your objective experience. If someone else was in the room with you, they would see the object also, though in their own way. You both would then compare your perception of the object and come to a consensual description about what's there. This is what we recognize and accept as objective public realty. The person in the room however would not be able to perceive your thoughts about the object. They are private, unseen by any public viewing.

PRACTICE 9

SEPARATING SUBJECT FROM OBJECT

Sit quietly and look at an object in the room. While you do this, let whatever thoughts and feelings you have associated with the object come to awareness.

As we discovered in Practice 8, our attention will move between the outer object and our inner associated experience about it. This is what attention does so well. It shines its light on both subject and object with equal facility.

Because our attention treats the outer object and our thoughts and feelings about the object as one unified field, it is up to us to make the distinction between the two.

As you sit looking at the object in the room, see if you can separate out your direct sensory perception of the object from your thoughts and feelings associated with it. In other words, what belongs to the object and what belongs to you.

FOURTH PRINCIPLE

WHAT YOU FOCUS ON BECOMES FOREGROUND IN YOUR FIELD OF PERCEPTION. WHAT YOU GIVE YOUR ATTENTION TO WILL BECOME THE CONTENT OF YOUR EXPERIENCE. YOU GET WHAT YOU FOCUS ON.

This principle is one of the most powerful tools we have for becoming self-aware and managing our state of being. Our ability to direct the focus of our attention, and thus create content from our field of perception, is the reason *why* we are learning to take control of our attention and make this process conscious instead of unconscious. Attending creates focus; focus creates content.

PRACTICE 10

CREATING FOREGROUND

Sit quietly and bring your attention into the room. Choose an object to focus on and watch how it appears vividly in your perception and becomes foreground in relationship to all other objects in the room. The other objects fall into the background and appear secondary, either falling away or becoming blurry or less distinct. Keep choosing different objects in the room to focus on until you see this process clearly.

PRACTICE 11

BEING IN YOUR HEAD

Let's expand this practice to include your entire field of awareness. Sit quietly and shift your attention into thought. Listen to the voice in your head, and observe any pictures that flash before the mind's eye. The more absorbed you become in thought, the less you will feel your body, and the less you will be aware of your surroundings. They will fall into the background while your inner dialogue and images take foreground. The common expression for this is being in your head.

PRACTICE 12

SHIFTING FOREGROUND AND BACKGROUND

Sit, relax, and let your attention drift freely. Let it focus where it may while you observe its movement. See if you can be aware of how foreground and background keep shifting from one moment to the next. This constant movement of perception is always in operation. Something is always being called forth as foreground, and something is always falling away as background.

FIFTH PRINCIPLE

ATTENTION REVEALS ITS OBJECT TO THE PERCEIVER WHILE KEEPING THE PERCEIVER UNKNOWN TO ITS SELF.

In normal everyday consciousness, we are organized to perceive in such a way that our attention is always focused on an object. We are always seeing, hearing, tasting, touching, smelling, feeling, thinking, or sensing something. When we are seeing something, we never see the looker, we only see what we are looking at. When we are hearing, we never hear the listener. The act of perceiving only illuminates what is perceived, not who the perceiver is.

PRACTICE 13

WHO IS LOOKING?

Do this right now. Lift your eyes from the page and scan the room you are in.

While seeing the objects in the room, can you also see who is doing the looking? Can you see the looker?

PRACTICE 14

WHO IS LISTENING?

1. Do this right now. Take a moment and think about Practice 13 from the preceding page. Listen to your thoughts and observe whether you can see or hear the listener. Who or what is hearing the thoughts?

2. The next time you find yourself listening to someone else, see if you can see or hear who is doing the listening. All you may be able to perceive is your own response, your thoughts and feelings about what is being said. Is this the listener?

It is one of the mysteries of our nature that we are wired to know the object of our attention without revealing the knower to ourselves. Just as physicists look into the heart of the atom and discover empty space, in our attempt to know ourselves, we must also peer into an invisible presence that appears to have no substance. This leaves us with the hint that our essence cannot be found in the content of our experience but in the awareness that holds it in place.

SIXTH PRINCIPLE

WHEN ATTENTION IS DIRECTED AT THE PERCEIVER, THE RESULT IS SELF-AWARENESS.

In order to become more self-aware, we must turn our attention inward and begin to explore the nature of our subjectivity. We must look behind outer events and the forms they take in order to understand how we work and come into being. When we do this, a new universe of experience opens up. We begin to see that the outer self we take ourselves to be is just part of a larger whole. Bringing attention under conscious control is our first step in becoming self-aware.

PRACTICE 15

MOVING INTO THOUGHT

1. Sit quietly with your eyes closed. As you sit, watch how your attention is drawn into thought once you have shut out the external world from your sight. Let this happen. After 30 seconds to a minute, open yours eyes again and let your attention move back out to your physical environment.

2. Repeat (1) again.

The path attention takes from perceiving our outer world to *being in thought* is a well travelled road. We spend most of our time moving between these two experiences. If we are not attending to our physical circumstance, we are thinking about it. We are constantly moving along the horizontal line between the outside world to the inner world of thought and back again. This is why when we close our eyes, we will most likely find ourselves drawn into thought. While it is a natural path for attention to take, it is not the only one available to be followed.

PRACTICE 16

UP AND DOWN

Sit quietly with your eyes closed. Instead of just looking and listening to your thoughts, shift your attention to a sensation in the body. Any sensation will do. Hold your attention on the sensation until you automatically move back into thought. Repeat this exercise for a few minutes, observing the movement back and forth.

Notice that the movement has a vertical axis. When you go into thought attention moves up, and when attention is given to sensation, it moves down into the body. Once this up and down movement becomes familiar to you, it will be easy to travel its path with a speed and clarity that makes centering in the body quick and effective.

Practices 1 through 16 were designed to give you experience in taking control of, and directing, your attention. We have been consciously exercising a muscle that is often underused. We direct our concentration all day long to the tasks at hand, but we seldom use this skill to direct it toward enhancing our state of being.

SKILL TWO

GROUNDING OURSELVES IN THE FACT OF THE BODY

Now that you have practice in taking control of your attention, let's practice exercising it in a way that will lead you deeper into the experience of greater self-awareness and a more expanded state of being. In order to do this, you must use your attention to ground yourself in the fact of the body. The phrase, *fact of the body*, represents the direct knowing experienced while in sensation, as compared to the symbolic nature of experience when in the mind. Continuing our process, we come to the last principle of attention.

SEVENTH PRINCIPAL

WHEN ATTENTION IS
FOCUSED ON IMMEDIATE FELT
EXPERIENCE, PERCEPTION
EXPANDS AND BECOMES MORE
COMPREHENSIVE—YOU BECOME
CENTERED, ALIGNED, EMBODIED
AND PRESENT.

PRACTICE 17

FROM SENSATION TO SENSING

While sitting quietly, let your right arm lay across your lap in front of you. Look at your arm and notice its size and shape. You are seeing your arm from the outside, like any other object in your immediate environment.

Now, with your eyes open, shift your attention so that you are feeling the arm. Shift from looking at it to feeling the sensation of the arm resting in your lap. Relax your shoulder and let the weight of the arm rest on your lap. If you start thinking about the arm, or catch yourself looking at it as an object, shift back to feeling the arm as sensation, feeling it from the inside out.

Now, see if you can look at the arm and sense the arm at the same time. When you can, you have now expanded your awareness of the arm to include both its outside and inside dimensions.

PRACTICE 18

ENERGETICS

Let's go back to the arm resting in your lap. With your eyes open, continue to focus your attention on the sensation of the arm. Stay there as best you can, feeling the arm *feel itself*. Stay there with presence, and you may begin to feel the cues that you are moving from sensation into sensing energy. The arm may feel warmer or cooler; it may feel tingly; it may feel heavier or lighter; you may feel as if there is something moving through it and around it. You may also lose the sense of the physical boundary of the arm and instead feel it expand and become more porous in feeling, as if it is disappearing.

All of these cues are signaling that you are in the process of shifting between the physical arm and the energy arm that exists around it and through it. You are changing your mode of perceiving from sensation, which is physical, to sensing, which is a more subtle yet equally valid way of knowing. Your perception will become subtler the longer your attention is able to rest in sense/felt experience.

PRACTICE 19

LOCATION AND DIMENSION

Sit quietly and shift your attention to your feet as they rest on the floor. Feel them in sensation.

Once you can feel your feet on the floor, add to your experience the sensation of feeling your seat in the chair. Feel the feet being supported by the floor and the body being supported by the chair.

Now add the feeling of your back resting against the back of the chair to your experience. Feel the support of being backed.

Hold these three sensory locations in awareness, your feet on the floor, your seat in the chair and your back against the back of the chair and relax into them.

As soon as you begin to experience the cues mentioned above (warmth, tingling, heaviness, loss of physical boundaries, etc.), acknowledge them as signs that you are entering a dimensional shift in perception. Keep doing what brought you to the shift – feeling your feet, feeling your seat in the chair and your back against the back of the chair.

You have now experienced the seventh principle in action. When attention is focused on immediate felt experience, perception expands and makes visible the next underlying reality that supports its existence. You achieve a more subtle perception of what is, a more multidimensional experience.

By focusing attention in the right location, e.g., body sensation, and holding it in awareness, you experience a dimensional shift in perception. Instead of attention continuing to move around within the same layer of experience, something opens up and the next layer is presented. Instead of continuing to move around, you begin to move within and through your experience.

PRACTICE 20

SETTLING DOWN

Sit quietly in a chair and bring attention to your feet, seat and back. Relax into these three points of sensation. As you practice settling into the fact of the body, it will become easier and more rapid to do—just a shift of attention away.

See if you notice a downward movement that makes you feel grounded and supported by an energy under and behind you. Pay attention to how the sensation of the physical body spreads out from these three points to include the entire body, as if body consciousness wants to feel itself as whole. When this occurs, simply rest in the experience and acknowledge the same cues you experienced with the arm practice. When the body is feeling itself as a whole, you will begin to experience a shift in perception to the energetic field that supports it.

By taking control of your attention and focusing on feet, seat and back, you are making contact with what supports you from under and behind, giving you a sense of ground. It also acts as a counterweight to the tendency to be pulled upward into thought. Instead of being pulled up and out of the connection with yourself, you can catch the deeper countermovement down and into yourself. With practice, these movements of up and down become recognized paths through which attention flows. You can choose to enter the movement consciously, and direct it toward a more expansive center of experience.

PRACTICE 21

FINDING A LARGER FOCUS

Sit quietly with your eyes closed. Settle into the body by feeling your feet, seat and back. Relax down through these three points of sensation. Keep settling until you can feel the body as a whole unit feeling itself. Rest in this sensation. Awareness of energetic cues will begin to appear: warmth, tingling, moving currents of energy, loss of physical boundaries, lightness or heaviness, and change in size. When this occurs, acknowledge these cues and continue to settle and accept them.

Staying with this sensed/felt experience, be alert to the following sensory cues: quiet and stillness, spaciousness and emptiness, a feeling of roundness or expanded size, and a feeling of being transparent. These are cues that you are experiencing a shift in consciousness and entering the field of energy and awareness that holds your mind and body within its field of perception.

PRACTICE 22

SITTINGS

Repeat Practice 21 on a regular basis until you can sit quietly and move through these shifts with some ease. Like developing any skill or art, it takes time and patience to become familiar with the experience you are cultivating. It takes practice and repetition to move your attention through different energy states and allow a shift in consciousness to occur.

This centered experience is the location from which to observe the mind/body relationship in action and manage your state of being more effectively. From here, you can generate the self-observation and self-awareness necessary to extricate yourself from being at the effect of your thoughts, feelings, circumstances and conditioned responses. This central location is also the doorway through which excursions into deeper states of consciousness can be taken. The same process of resting within a state with full presence will open and make visible the next dimension of consciousness that is waiting to be explored.

PRACTICE 23

FROM THINKING TO RECEIVING

Sit quietly, and as you shift from thought, to body, to energy field, count to 100 verbally inside your head. When you get to 50, instead of just hearing yourself counting in your head, switch to an image of the numbers counting off in front of you. When you reach 100, start the counting again by either hearing them or seeing them before the mind's eye. If at any time you begin to hear or see the numbers counting by themselves, you will know you are in a receptive state and doing a good job of stepping away from controlling content. This is a good place from which to observe the mind and the mind/body connection in operation. You are not driving the action but allowing it to unfold on its own. This is the beginning of receiving self-experience instead of generating it.

PRACTICE 24

SITTING WITH AWARENESS

Sit quietly with your eyes closed. Settle into the body by feeling your feet, seat and back. Relax down through these three points of sensation. Keep settling until you can feel the body as a whole unit feeling itself.

Give your attention to relaxing your hold on the content that shows up. Observe the propensity for your attention to be directed by the mind's interest in the content. Content can be any thought, image, feeling or sensation that appears within your awareness.

Begin to give more attention to the sensed/felt space that your awareness appears to occupy. Content will continue to show up. However, allow your attention to become more interested and involved in the sensed/felt experience of spaciousness and volume that surrounds and contains whatever content arises. Let the boundaries of this space expand.

PRACTICE 25

OUTER LOOKING VERSUS INNER SEEING

LOOKING

Sit quietly and look at an object in the room. Give your full attention to the object. Notice how your attention goes out to, covers, and surrounds the object. You, the perceiver, and the object, the perceived, appear to be separate.

SEEING

Settle into the body. Instead of letting your attention seek out the object, remain centered and expand your awareness until you are seeing the object with your eyes, and feeling it with your body. This may feel like the object is being drawn to you, instead of your attention going out to the object.

Looking at something removes you from yourself, while *seeing* joins you with the object. Looking is one-dimensional, while seeing is multidimensional. Seeing joins the sight of the eyes with the sight/sense of the body, creating a larger and deeper state of knowing.

What results is a more intimate and comprehensive relationship with whatever is being held in perception. It is only in the last 50 years that the western world has dis-covered that the body itself can perceive and know, and is informed by many subtle bodies. We now use the term energetic to designate this kind or state of knowing.

PRACTICE 26

PLAYING IN THE ENERGY FIELD

Sit quietly with your eyes closed. Settle into the body by feeling your feet, seat and back. Relax down through these three points of sensation. Keep settling until you can feel the body as a whole unit feeling itself. Rest in this state of sensation until it shifts into a larger energy field that is spacious, quiet and still.

Within this field is a center vertical line like the spine of the physical body. See if you can sense/feel these two vertical lines—the centerline of the energy field, and the spine of the body – aligned and occupying the same vertical space. Light may begin to fill the space. Allow it to generate an even more expanded state.

PRACTICE 27

WHAT ARE YOU DOING WHILE YOU'RE DOING WHAT YOU'RE DOING?

Bringing self-awareness into daily life now becomes an arena for play and exploration. Every outer action you perform and every behavior you express in the world is an opportunity for practice. Activities like walking, talking, driving, relating to a friend and doing your job all have an inner component to them. While performing these actions on the outside, you can be settling into the fact of the body on the inside, using the resulting shifts in perception to become more present and to deepen your appreciation of the moment.

Some places to play:

1. Before starting the engine of your car, settle into the seat and sense/feel your energetic connection to the car.

2. In conversations with intimates or workmates, notice and feel any energetic movements in your body that are evoked in response to their words.

3. While walking, settle into your feet and legs and try to feel the source of power that supports your movement through space.

4. In the midst of an emotion, experience its movement through the body as an energy flow.

5. While exercising in the gym, use each repetition in your routine to feel the body from the inside instead of looking at it from the outside.

6. When in nature, settle into your body and feel your energetic connection to your surroundings.

SKILL THREE

RELEASING OURSELVES FROM THE FICTION OF THE MIND

Now that you are actively using your attention to create your state and to ground yourself in the fact of the body, let's look at the third skill that will support your becoming self-aware: releasing yourself from the fiction of the mind. It is important to put the mind in its proper place or it will dominate the movement and direction of your experience. To accomplish this, you must first be curious to see what role it plays in the construction of your current state of being. There are four assumptions that will guide our practice.

ASSUMPTION ONE

THOUGHT AND FEELING ARE CONNECTED

The conscious mind represents itself to us through the images and voice dialog that we see and hear in our head. These images and inner dialogues give us the field of meaning and interpretation that the emotional body uses to release emotional energy into our conscious awareness. To see if this is true, we will use our first two skills to create the best location from which to observe this process.

PRACTICE 28

JOINING THOUGHT AND FEELING

Sit quietly and settle into the body. Feel your feet on the floor, your seat in the chair and your back against the back of the chair. When you feel you are grounded in sensation, call up a memory that is painful.

Observe what happens emotionally in the body as you hold this memory in awareness.

Now let go and sit quietly and settle into the body. Feel your feet on the floor, your seat in the chair and your back against the back of the chair. When you feel you are grounded in sensation, call up a memory that is joyful.

Observe what happens in sensation in the body as you hold this memory in awareness.

Bringing these images and narratives to conscious awareness activates energetic movement within our body. If we remove the mind's judgment about whether this movement is good or bad, painful or pleasurable, we see that it is simply a movement that responds to the thoughts we entertain.

By doing these simple, everyday actions with embodied awareness, you will see how thought and feeling are related and how they impact your state in the moment.

When you join thought with emotional feeling, you create a more comprehensive experience of self, a larger field of experience, observation and awareness. Your ideas and emotional energy are joined in your awareness. You can now simultaneously receive your thoughts and feelings, which expands your experience and begins the process of skillfully managing your state of being.

ASSUMPTION TWO

YOUR INTERPRETATION CREATES YOUR RESPONSE

Your mind is the repository of all your past decisions concerning the nature of your particular reality. It delivers up this information in the form of stories you tell yourself as you confront present experience. These fixed points of view give you the lens through which you interpret the meaning of any moment and justify your responses as being true and right.

This ability to create meaning is a wonderful tool for making sense out of the immense amount of sensory information available to you. However, if your responses are left unexamined in the face of ever-changing direct experience, they become unconscious and dominate your view and form your reactions. Your stories thus become a liability when elevated to the position of belief and truth, and you accept into awareness only what fits the narrative. You are then left with diminished awareness instead of an expansion of your reality.

PRACTICE 29

FILLING IN THE WORLD

1. Observe one of your characteristic behaviors and then listen to how you justify it as necessary. The story you tell yourself will be the carrier of a belief you hold.

Example:

Behavior—I can become angry and aggressive when I think I am being criticized.

Justification—I have been unfairly blamed and misunderstood.

Belief—No one else can see me as clearly as I see myself.

2. Identify a feeling that you carry or revisit with some frequency. Stop it in its motion and feel it. Become present to it. As you feel into it, listen for the voices that are connected to it and the story they weave. The belief will be in the story about the feeling.

Example:

Feeling—I feel unsafe and vulnerable.

Story – I must be vigilant and cautious around people because I can't control what they may do.

Belief—People are basically untrustworthy.

3. Write down a judgment you have of yourself. Now write down the story you tell yourself about why you are this way.

Example:

Judgment—I am too afraid of making a mistake.

Story—When I was young my mother was always sharp and demanding of me. This made me expect to be reprimanded when things went wrong.

4. Write down a criticism of someone close to you and your explanation as to why they are the way you see them. What does your story about them reveal about *you*?

Example:

Criticism – My friend John is too needy.

Story – Because he received little attention from his parents growing up, he keeps trying to get it from his friends now.

Me – I believe that it shows weakness to openly express your needs.

In the absence of direct knowledge or experience, the mind will fill in the blanks. I have called this action filling in the world. When you are faced with an unknown, the mind fills it with what is already known. You fill in the world with your conditioning, not your creative imagination. This response is driven by the ego, whose purpose is to support the self-image you are committed to and already know. We are all subject to this unconscious conditioning, which is often the cause of our suffering.

PRACTICE 30

BREAKING UP STORY

Pen and paper exercise:

1) Write down a story you tell yourself about why you are the way you are.

Example:

My parents neglected me as a child and as a result I don't look to others for support and nurturing.

2) As a consequence of filling in the world about yourself in this way, how does it make you feel? Write down your response.

Example:

I feel alone and under appreciated.

3) Given this feeling, what behavior toward yourself does it elicit from you? Write down your response.

Example:

I neglect my own needs.

4) If you stopped filling in the world about yourself in this way, what new feeling might emerge in you? Write down your response.

Example:

An open heartedness for being joined.

5) If this new feeling was present, what new behavior would it elicit from you toward yourself? Write down your response.

Example:

A more direct expression of my needs from others.

6) What has this process revealed to you about yourself? Review your responses above and write down your observation.

Example:

I see that my belief in my story keeps me fixed and separates me from experiencing what I truly desire.

PRACTICE 31

OUTSIDE THE BOX

Pen and paper exercise:

1. Choose a train of thought or story that you carry about yourself that diminishes you when you listen to it. Write it down the way you hear it in your mind.

Example:

Be careful how much of yourself you expose, you run the risk of being criticized and rejected.

2. Now turn it into its positive opposite.

Example:

I am willing to be open about myself and expect to be accepted just the way I am.

3. What does this statement make possible?

Example:

A loving feeling of acceptance of myself and an eagerness to share my experience.

4. How would you feel if that possibility were true? Feel it and write down your experience.

Example:

Big, open and excited.

5. What behavior or actions would you perform if this possibility was realized? Write them down.

Example:

I would share myself more freely and invite others into my life with more enthusiasm.

6. What new thoughts would support this new experience? Write them down.

Example:

I can trust people to accept me.

Making my thoughts and feelings visible to others is fulfilling instead of dangerous.

There is joy in expressing myself regardless of whether I am accepted or not.

PRACTICE 32

MAKING HIDDEN BELIEFS VISIBLE

You can use this practice to uncover any beliefs that lie hidden within any issue you may be experiencing. To illustrate its use, I have included the responses of a student, in italics, who ran this process in class regarding her issue: not feeling free to express herself. After reading through the exercise, replace this example with the issue you wish to explore and run the process for yourself.

Pen and paper exercise:

1. Write down three beliefs or perceptions you have about the world that (state issue) ...

Our example: The world inhibits my willingness to express myself.

They won't understand me.

The world is uninterested in what I have to say.

The world will punish me for what I have to say.

2. Take each statement you made about the world and find and extract a belief or perception you have about yourself from it.

I am not good at making myself understood.

I am not interesting or qualified enough to be listened to.

I have thoughts and feelings that need to be hidden or they will get me in trouble.

3. Take the first, second and third statements from your first response and pair them with the first, second and third statements from your second response.

They won't understand me.

I am not good at making myself understood.

The world is uninterested in what I have to say.

I am not interesting enough to be listened to.

The world will punish me for what I have to say.

I have thoughts and feelings that need to be hidden or they will get me in trouble.

Remember these are beliefs you have created from conclusions you have arrived at in the past. They are fiction, but masquerade as fact in your mind, and therefore have emotional support in the body. Once they are elevated to belief, they are assigned to your baseline view of reality, and become resistant to being tested against your current direct experience.

4. What is the characteristic train of thought you hear in your head that represents each pairing?

They won't understand me.

I am not good at making myself understood.

<u>*What I hear in my head*</u>—*Why bother, they won't really understand me.*

The world is uninterested in what I have to say.

I am not interesting or qualified enough to be listened to.

<u>*What I hear in my head*</u>*—Why make any effort, it's not important what I think or feel.*

The world will punish me for what I have to say.

I have thoughts and feelings that need to be hidden or they will get me in trouble.

<u>*What I hear in my head*</u>*—Better watch out what you say, they'll get upset.*

5. Take each train of thought statement and reduce it to a one-word emotional or behavioral stance.

Indifference

Withholding

Hidden

In this case, these are conditioned inhibitors that diminish this person's will to speak.

6. Reverse each of these into their positive counterpart.

Caring

Giving

Being seen

7. From the positive counterpart above, create a declarative I statement for each inhibitor that represents a desire or willingness on your part.

I care if you hear me.

I want to give of myself freely.

I want you to see me.

Once these beliefs are distilled and broken down to this last statement, you experience the vulnerability they were initially created to protect.

What surfaced in this particular example was an original desire for connection that was there before a conceptual way of protecting the self from its perceived absence was generated.

After you go through your process you can then embrace and work with the new ideas and images that were generated. The ones you began with were born out of resistance against an invisible force of your own making. This process reveals that expansion and possibility are only a thought away. It shows us that when our pictures and images change, our feelings and state of being also are altered. It also shows us the degree to which we are at the effect of our own thinking. As the thought goes, so do we. As we experience release from the fiction of the mind, we can entertain thought without becoming subject to it. We become free enough and safe enough to play with thought creatively, in a way that is *for* us instead of *against* us.

ASSUMPTION THREE

YOUR USE OF TIME DETERMINES YOUR SENSE OF POWER

In everyday consciousness, we experience ourselves as subject to linear time. We believe and act as if the present is just a stopping place between where we've been and where we're going. For us, the past and the future are just as real as the present moment. We believe this because the past and the future occur so vividly in our mind's eye. Sometimes we can see them as clearly as if they were actually happening right now. We forget that the mind is offering a concept in the form of symbol, image or narrative, not a direct experience.

PRACTICE 33

THE MIND IS TIME

Sit quietly and settle into the body. Feel your feet on the floor, your seat in the chair and your back against the back of the chair. When you feel like you are present in the body, answer the following questions:

1. How successful do you expect to be in the coming year? (Prediction)

2. How do you plan to spend your next vacation and what do you think it will be like? (Anticipation)

3. Imagine a decision you want to make but are refraining from making. What do you see happening to you if you make it? (Perceived consequences)

Prediction, anticipation and perceived consequences are some of the ways the mind delivers the future to us. If we don't recognize that we are using time to create fiction, we will take our pictures as fact and organize our state, as well as our life around them.

4. Think of someone you know to whom you want to say something, but have withheld saying or sharing it. Write down what you think their response would be if you shared it.

Do you use this assessment to determine whether to say something to them or not?

What feeling does your assessment evoke in you when you entertain this train of thought?

Does this feeling support or obstruct your decision process?

5. Think of a future situation or event in which you are planning to participate. Write down a brief description of what you think it will be like when you experience it.

What expectation does this prediction create in you?

Does this prediction influence how willing you are to participate in this future event?

In what way does it do this?

PRACTICE 34

THE PAST AND FUTURE HAVE US

Sit quietly and experience a past hurt without using thought. Can this be done?

Sit quietly and experience a future excitement without using thought. Can this be done?

Make a list of three possible choices that are present in your life at this time, choices waiting to be made. How many of these choices can you make without reference to past or future?

The past and future do not exist except as thought. When we realize this, we free ourselves from mistaking fiction as fact. We can then use our symbolic, thought based life to support and expand the present self. The past and future can now be used in a creative way that was not possible before.

PRACTICE 35

THE PRESENT SERVES THE PAST

Pen and paper exercise:

1. Write down a short description of a memory that has an emotional charge or impact on you when you evoke it. (It can be a positive or negative memory.)

Example: I am talking with my parents on the phone about them picking me up from boarding school for the weekend. My parents tell me they are not coming. I look over and see another kid crying because his parents aren't going to pick him up either. I feel alone and abandoned.

2. What is the feeling that the memory evokes in you?

Example: I feel afraid and lonely.

3. What idea, inner narrative or story is associated with this feeling?

Example: I am not safe and secure in the world, and I cannot trust those closest to me to be there for me. They will turn on me.

4. What declarative statement can be distilled from this combination of thought and feeling?

Example: I am afraid that if I am bad I will be deserted.

5. What function does this belief serve in your current experience?

Example: To keep what I think is bad hidden.

6. Does this belief achieve its intended purpose? If not, what does it achieve? Does this contract or expand your current experience?

Example: No, it keeps me separate and small.

7. Make a declarative statement that represents your commitment to this belief.

Example: I am committed to being small and separate.

PRACTICE 36

THE PAST SERVES THE PRESENT

This practice demonstrates the constructive use of memory. Our memories are a pool of collective stories that are always being reinvented by the current self. Our recollections are not necessarily accurate reflections of what took place in the moment of their creation. They have been at the service of every version of you from then until now, forever being reinvented to serve the intention of the self for its own purpose. When this is recognized, we can choose to use the past more constructively, not to undermine ourselves, but to support ourselves into being.

Pen and Paper exercise:

1. Think of a current desire you have which, if you had the right thought and feeling to support it, you would act upon. What is the desire?

2. Now go into your memory and find two circumstances or past experiences that support this desire.

3. As you reflect on these past experiences and their relationship to your current desire, what do you feel?

4. Does the memory of this past experience, both in thought and feeling, now make it more possible for you to act in regard to this desire?

5. Sit in the energy of the feeling that is evoked by the combination of your memory of the past and your current desire.

6. Remain in this feeling and let images come to you that represent the successful completion of this current desire. See it happening in a probable future.

PRACTICE 37

CONSTRUCTIVE USE
OF THE FUTURE

We are either subject to time or users of time. When we are subject to time, the past is used to describe what is *real and possible* for us and thus constrains any future possibilities. When we grant ourselves permission to consciously use the mind and its fictions in the service of ourselves, we become *constructive users* of time and thus become powerful and creative players in our own experience.

Pen and paper exercise:

Pick a future event that you are planning and anticipating will happen. Write down what you expect to happen based on using and applying constructive memory. In other words, be selective and creative in the way you draw from your conditioned pool of past information. Support your future vision so that it will then flow back and support the current self and its actions.

ASSUMPTION FOUR

THE MOVEMENT OF CONTRACTION AND EXPANSION GENERATES THE QUALITY OF YOUR STATE.

All day long we are subjected to the movement of expansion and contraction as the mind makes its interpretations and the body responds as if they are true, real and immediate. Depending on the particular interpretation, we then contract or expand in energy, and feel closed or open.

PRACTICE 38

OBSERVING CONTRACTION AND EXPANSION IN ACTION

Pen and paper exercise:

All of the questions below have been designed to demonstrate the connection between mind and body and the energy they produce that gives shape, size and texture to your state in the moment.

Sit quietly and settle into the body. Feel your feet on the floor, your seat in the chair and your back against the back of the chair. When you feel like you are present to sensation, respond to each question separately. Feel the energetic response to each question in your body before moving on to the next. Be curious and interested in observing your self contract and expand in relation to your answers.

1. What *thoughts* do you have about your life that lead you to contract? Find two and write them down.

2. What *thoughts* do you have about your life that lead you to expand? Find two and write them down.

3. What *feelings* do you have about your life that cause you to contract? Find two and write them down.

4. What *feelings* of expansion do you avoid or control? Find two and write them down.

5. Think of a future event you are anticipating. Envision it happening now and observe how this affects you.

6. Think of a choice you would like to make but are not making. Prepare yourself to make it now. What do you feel?

As you can see, meaning is delivered to the mind, the mind delivers it to the body, and our subtle body responds by closing down or opening up. We are always living within this moving field of contracting and expanding energy.

PRACTICE 39

TRANSFORMING THREAT INTO POSSIBILITY

Pen and paper exercise:

1. Choose a fearful train of thought that diminishes you when you entertain it. Write it down the way you hear it in your head.

2. Turn it into its opposite positive statement. What does this statement make possible?

3. How would you feel if the possible were true? Feel it.

4. Choose which feeling or energy you wish to use as a platform for action and manifestation—the fiction that has contracted you, or the possibility that opens you.

PRACTICE 40

PLAYING FREELY WITH SYMBOLS

If thoughts are merely symbols, what stops us from playing with them freely? It is our belief that they are facts, that they represent a truth, and that they have substance beyond what we give them.

1. Take a desire that you have and entertain it in thought. Remember that thought shows up as voice narrative and visual images.

2. Write down what stops you from playing freely with these narratives and images?

3. Now take control of the imaging process and move it in the direction that, in your wildest imagination, you would like it to go. What happens in feeling and thought when you do this?

ADDITIONAL SUGGESTIONS
FOR LIFE PRACTICE

The following are some suggestions to assist you in bringing a deeper awareness to the role that contraction and expansion plays in determining the quality of your state at any given moment.

1. When you find yourself in a state of contraction; i.e., in fear, depression, hurt, disappointment, resentment or resignation; see if you can feel the cues present in the body that identify this state. What is happening in and through your body energetically?

2. When you find yourself contracted, observe the degree of *permission* you grant yourself for experiencing it in the moment. Also, look to see how much permission there is for expressing it into your world; i.e., as verbal or behavioral interaction with others.

3. When you are feeling good, joyful, happy, or peaceful, notice if the experience has a self-imposed limit attached to it. Is there a line in your experience that would be wrong or dangerous for you or others to cross? What is the belief you hold that would be violated if you surrendered to your expansive feeling in the moment?

4. When contracted, see if you can hear the justification you speak to yourself for continuing to stay contracted.

Is the justification directed at yourself, at others or at life circumstances?

5. Even when you feel contracted, the energy present in the contraction wants to continue its movement toward expansion. See if you can identify whom you are protecting from the movement of this energy – Are you protecting yourself or those around you?

6. Generally speaking, our reaction to the energy of contraction is to avoid or deny it. Our reaction to expansion is to contain or modify it to fit within what we consider appropriate boundaries. See if you can observe or uncover the inner dialogue or pictures that create these two responses in you.

7. When you find yourself in a contraction brought on by the presence of apprehension, you are most likely taking a response in the moment and running it into the future. That response then comes back to you in the form of fear. See if you can feel your fear without generating a future linked to it.

8. Anger itself is not a contraction but a response to one. When you feel the beginning of a contraction that is unacceptable to you; e.g., feeling small or powerless; you may call up anger or power to avoid the contraction. See if you can observe this dynamic when angry. In energy, something that feels small is attempting to make itself big.

9. How does an imagined threat become a fact? See if you can observe yourself in the following action:

   a) The mind presents an interpretation or fictional picture to your awareness.

b) The body accepts it as fact, and responds as if it is happening now.

c) The body's response does not differentiate between direct sensory experience and imagination, or between past, present and future.

d) If *you* are not making these distinctions consciously, your state of being goes into contraction.

e) The feeling of contraction in the body provides proof to the mind that something is wrong, and justifies further belief or evidence for the validity of the threat, which is now perceived as fact.

10. When you find yourself afraid, acknowledge your experience instead of resisting it. Move attention into immediate felt experience. Settle into the body and come to ground, or use your physical senses to locate yourself in space. Ground your experience in the here and now.

Now recognize that you are accepting fiction as fact. You are accepting a thought pattern based on past conditioning as an accurate prediction of future events. Once you recognize that you are dealing with thought, evoke the possibility process from Practice 39. Turn contraction into expansion and allow the energy of the contraction to move.

You now have a better understanding and awareness of how the mind and body are connected, and how they cooperate in producing the movement of opening and closing, feeling tight and feeling loose, feeling small and feeling big. With this awareness comes the possibility for being more proactive in generating the state you want to experience. You can ride the energy of this movement more gracefully by staying embodied as it moves through you. As a result you are free to choose the thoughts that will evoke the feelings you want to experience. You now have the skill to use the fiction of the mind in a conscious, creative way.

I have taken you through a linear process of practices. However, learning about your self from yourself is a multi-dimensional process. As we have seen, time and space are merely part of the mechanics of experience that we use to put ourselves together. By opening yourself to becoming self-aware, all parts of the self will now cooperate to support your growth.

Continue to practice taking control of your attention, grounding yourself in the fact of the body, and releasing yourself from the fiction of the mind. This practice will guide you on your way, and put you in a position to receive further instruction directly from your own process of becoming self-aware.

Practicing the three skills brings you into alignment with your emerging self experience in the moment, allowing you to play a more creative role in its unfolding. You can now process your thoughts and feelings with more discernment and authenticity and transform your relationship with them from being at their effect to using them creatively to produce the experience you most deeply desire.

This alignment leads you into a profound new attunement with the subtle energies that exist just below your ordinary consciousness and produces a more expanded perception of the field of energy and awareness that you inhabit. Gaining access to the wisdom and guidance that is available at this subtler level of your self moves you into a multidimensional relationship with the source of vision, inspiration and revelation that has always been informing your life and now becomes an active conscious partnership.

This relationship will guide you and position you within your experience to learn about your self from yourself as a continuous lifelong process, an engagement that will generate meaning, vitality and an ever deepening clarity to see through the mystery of who you are and why you are here.

GLOSSARY

Attention – Our capacity to focus, point, target and illuminate the object under our gaze. It is the creative instrument we use to construct our state of being, and is the active dynamic that determines what we perceive at any given moment.

Alignment – When our conceptual, sensate, and energetic experiences are joined in awareness, producing a more comprehensive experience of self.

Attunement – Sharing the same energetic frequency with an object, person or larger state of consciousness. Being equal in harmonic resonance facilitates the experience of becoming one with it and allows for shifts in one's state. It is the central means by which we are able to move through the subtle energies that make up our subjective, interior universe.

Alternate Focus – When attention is released from its concentration on habitual forms and becomes free to roam beyond the limits imposed by ordinary waking consciousness.

Baseline Frequency – A feeling state that we naturally gravitate toward and rest in. It is a felt sense of ourselves, generated from the inside, which is the touchstone we always return to as a natural consequence of living in the pull of conceptual gravity.

Committed Visitor – We are committed by birth to physical existence and the laws that govern its mechanics. This is our objective stance in the world and its laws dictate how the surface of things move and relate. At the same time, we are visitors who are not bound subjectively to these mechanics. We transcend them daily by traveling within our subjective universe, exiting time and space in sleep, dreams, imagination and all the subtle shifts of consciousness that place us outside its influence.

Conceptual Gravity –A force that draws our awareness to a baseline consciousness (vibration or feeling) to which we habitually return. When we are not conscious and active in choosing our state in the moment, this force, consisting of our unexamined beliefs, pulls us to reside at our baseline frequency.

Consciousness – The creative force that underlies all manifest forms. It is the creative medium that allows inner meaning to translate itself into outer form.

Conscious Evolution of Consciousness – A joint process whereby the inner self presents new material to the mind and opens up the mind to explore new possibilities for being. This cooperative and creative relationship is either translating energy into different forms or giving birth to new ones.

Contraction and Expansion –A movement set in motion by our every act of perception. The mind brings its interpretation and meaning to the moment and the body responds as if the assessment is true, real and immediate

Dynamic Reciprocity – A giving and receiving that joins all levels of the self. Each level of consciousness gives and receives, acts upon and is acted upon, and is held together by an empathic bond.

Embodiment – When attention is fully focused on and resting in the sense/felt experience of the body.

Energetic Awareness – A subtle dimension of experience that is perceived by the body. It produces images and information through a form of perceiving that is sensed and felt as compared to thought.

Fact of the Body – While a fact is usually defined as being objective in nature, body sensation is a universal subjective fact, one that can be relied on to be ever present when we turn our attention to it. Because the body never moves out of the present moment, the fact of the body is the ground from which we can travel into thought or into the world and yet still return to ourselves

Fiction of the Mind – The mind's inherent capacity and function to build narrative story and mental images out of direct sensory experience.

Field of Energy and Awareness Beyond the Mind/ Body – A state of consciousness one experiences as a consequence of having attention fully focused on the sense/felt experience of the body. Its typical qualities are a profound sense of silence, stillness and spaciousness. One has the experience of being separate from the action and motion of their mind and body, shifting one's identity to the field like presence that contains them.

Filling in the World –The propensity of the conscious mind, when faced with the unknown or unfamiliar, to fill the vacuum with what is already known. The mind will draw from its pool of past knowledge, experience and beliefs to make sense of the present experience, disregarding the novelty of direct experience and the need to generate new interpretations.

Hold and Release – A movement that is initiated by the presence of conceptual gravity. We are held to the self we know by our old ideas and stories, always returning to the familiar experience of ourselves with its characteristic feelings, thoughts and points of view. At the same time, we are released from the familiar when we experience moments of intuitive knowing, insight, vision, inspiration and revelation that transform our experience to a new level of perception.

Horizontal Axis of Awareness – The implicit direction that attention takes from self to world and back again.

Inhabiting your Essence – An experience where we are occupying and living in a state of self-awareness.

Multi-dimensional Experience – Distinguishing many layers of experience simultaneously. This capacity is central to meditation practice and is instrumental in allowing shifts in consciousness.

Our Story – The continuous stream of mental interpretation and comment offered by the mind. It is the constant verbal conversation that goes on within our minds and the internal out-picturing projected before the mind's eye.

Perceptual Integration – A creative action within consciousness where divergent aspects of the self come into alignment and attunement and join to produce an expansion in perception and a shift in the state of the perceiver.

Point of Perception – When attention is grounded in the here and now, recognizing the point of emergent experience as perceptual in nature that gives feedback about the nature and form of our present state.

Self-Awareness – The capacity we are born with to observe and reflect on the content of our experience.

State of Being – One's subjective world, filled with all the thoughts, feelings, sensations and energetic subtleties of one's conscious experience and the perceived moment of its unfolding.

State of Self-Awareness—An experience of consciously occupying the moment of emergent experience, leading to conscious knowledge of one's nature.

The Current – An experience of being infused through the body with energy that illuminates thought and feeling with insight and revelatory content.

Vertical Axis of Awareness – The implicit direction that attention takes as it moves up and down between sensation/feeling to thought and back again.

ACKNOWLEDGEMENTS

I am indebted to all those who supported me in the process of writing this book.

Gratitude to my friend, Pierre Delattre, for his many readings of the manuscript and his encouragement to continue. Thanks to Warren Bellows for his support and creative input concerning content and aesthetic design.

Many thanks to my readers: Laureen Asato, Beth Blach, Russell Delman, Elizabeth Helms, Amy Lansky, Silvia Reischl, Bruce Rohrer and Denise Treu for reading and offering feedback that made this a better book.

I am deeply appreciative and grateful to my dear friend and editor, Marcia Taylor, for making my prose more accessible without losing my meaning and voice. You truly brought the ship to harbor.

Thanks to all of my friends and students through the years who shared with me the wonder and joy of evolving our consciousness by becoming self-aware.

My deep appreciation to my ongoing study group who have been the living laboratory for validating the concepts and practices outlined in this book: Laureen Asato, Beth Blach, Jen Bulik, Susanne Dern, Jon Freeman, Shirley Grant, Elizabeth Helms, Lynne Klaeveman, Katie Koralek, Jeff Lang, Amy Lansky, Jean Marinovich, Bruce Rohrer, Hazel Simon, Denis Treu and Michael Temkin.

Lastly and most importantly, I am forever thankful to the love and joy of my life, my wife Ellen Miller, who joined me every step of the way in exploring the nature of becoming self-aware and without whose help and support this book could not have been written.

THE AUTHOR

GARY SHERMAN has been a psychotherapist and teacher of self-awareness and meditation for over four decades. As an educator and teacher he is committed to exploring our deepest human potential and translating the results into practical knowledge that can be used to elevate our lives. He designs and delivers classes, workshops, programs, and curriculums teaching self-awareness, expanded perception and inner growth.

He is the originator of Perceptual Integration an educational process for training others in becoming self-aware. He is co-founder of the Creative Awareness Project in Santa Rosa, California and co-author with Ellen Miller of *Silence and the Soul: Awakening Inner Wisdom.* He and his partner, Ellen, live in Sonoma County, California.

CPSIA information can be obtained at www.ICGtesting.com
Printed in the USA
BVOW08s1154081113

335770BV00003B/3/P